Bryn Mawr Latin Commentaries

Editors

Julia Haig Gaisser
Bryn Mawr College

James J. O'Donnell
University of Pennsylvania

The purpose of the Bryn Mawr Latin Commentaries is to make a wide range of classical and post-classical authors accessible to the intermediate student. Each commentary provides the minimum grammatical and lexical information necessary for a first reading of the text.

The Bryn Mawr Latin Commentaries are supported by a
generous grant from the Division of Education Programs of
the National Endowment for the Humanities

Manufactured in the United States of America

ISBN 0-929524-76-4

Printed and distributed by:
Bryn Mawr Commentaries
Thomas Library
Bryn Mawr College
101 North Merion Avenue
Bryn Mawr, PA 19010-2899

Medieval Latin Lyric

Volume 1

Penelope Rainey

Thomas Library
Bryn Mawr College

Table of Contents

Preface

This selection of medieval Latin song and verse is intended to give as wide a picture of shorter medieval poetry in Latin as possible in a relatively short scope. Hymns and any longer poems that would have had to be excerpted do not appear here. Ranging in date from *ca.* 500 - 1300 A.D., the selections are deliberately varied in content and form and are intended to represent the major types of shorter poems or songs of the various medieval periods. Even so, the selections scarcely succeed in adequately representing the variety and richness of medieval poetry.

The Latin poetry of the Middle Ages is a very complex phenomenon. It is a fusion of classical and Biblical language, themes, and imagery—a fascinating synthesis of Christian belief and classical rhetoric. At the same time, it is the product of the developing language and culture of medieval Latin, in many ways very distinct from Classical language, literature, and culture. Medieval Latin was the written and spoken Latin of the clerical and, sometimes, the aristocratic classes. The popular cultures and the vernacular languages of western Europe colored its content, in ways on which scholars do not agree. Though the language (Latin) of all the verse of this collection implies some learning, the quality of the learning, and of the influence of classical Latin, varies (cf. No. 9). Many selections represent the clear influences of popular song, e.g., Nos. 6, 11, 13. However, the Latin poetry and the vernacular poetry of the Middle Ages do not belong to separate categories. They overlap in themes, tone, and imagery (especially in the case of courtly love poetry), and they share many of the same musical forms. Overall, though there were differences of literary expression in the different regions of Europe, medieval Latin poetry bears witness to a common European cultural tradition.

The richness of medieval poetry is also apparent in the close interconnection between secular and religious lyric that is typical of the Middle Ages. Few distinctions of authorship, form, audience, or language can be drawn between the religious and the secular. Clerics, as the only educated members of early medieval society, were originally the sole authors of Latin verse, secular as well as religious, and the preservers of any early vernacular poetry we still have. In the later Middle Ages, membership in the church was still the usual *sine qua non* of scholarship and learning, and Latin still the *lingua franca* of the clerical and aristocratic classes. Though with the development of a bourgeois class the vernacular languages and literatures became increasingly important, teaching at the universities was still exclusively clerical, and its language, Latin, still the dominant medium of exchange for a shared European culture.

Many of the selections of this collection are songs of which the first "publication" was a performance. Music was a crucial part of the effect of most medieval lyrics. If we read these works without taking account of their musical dimensions, we clearly miss a part of their artistic meaning. (Recently, excellent recordings of medieval music have become available, and these should be consulted.) Furthermore, many were addressed to a particular audience, whose reactions would be immediate. The poet/singer doubtless frequently improvised on the instant—thus creating many of the textual variants that still puzzle scholars.

In this collection, a short commentary introduces each poem, intended to summarize the historical and cultural context and to give some biographical information for the author, if known. The notations on the manuscripts of each poem are designed to indicate major textual problems and to give some hint of the challenge and difficulty of determining the texts of these poems. Instead of an *apparatus criticus*, important textual differences are indicated in the line notes. The brief metrical information given for each selection should be supplemented by the appendix "Medieval Verse Technique." The bibliography cited for each poem is only intended to give the major editions and one or two contemporary, relevant articles or books. Abbreviations of frequently cited works can be found in the "Bibliography of Works often Cited."

The reader should consult line notes and the "Linguistic Note" for difficult or interesting discrepancies in morphology and syntax between medieval and classical Latin. The reader should not expect the orthography to be consistent. The best modern editions exhibit considerable variety of practice among themselves—and no medieval reader, glancing through manuscripts of different dates and provenances, would have been surprised by any lack of consistency.

Penelope Rainey
The Germantown Friends School
October 1992

Linguistic Note

As a result of a variety of causes—the greater influence of spoken Latin on written Latin in the era of the later empire where general education was declining, changing populations within the empire and the influx of new populations and languages from outside the empire, the bureaucratic "officialese" of late imperial administration, the necessity for a new, "Christian" vocabulary—Medieval Latin is in many ways very different from literary, classical Latin. Even the fact that ML did develop tendencies already present in Silver Age literary Latin as well as in spoken Latin does not change this difference. Recurrent "classical renaissances" (e.g., in the 9th or 12th centuries) did not totally reverse the development of this new type of Latin. However, ML was not monolithic: there was great regional variation in the language, especially in the early Middle Ages; some authors were much more "classically" trained than others.

Orthography. The many variations in ML spelling often reflect new pronunciations, though sometimes merely a poor knowledge of Latin. Consistency in determining a writer's orthography is very difficult, because even when the writers themselves were consistent, scribes and modern editors "correct," often haphazardly.
1.   Variation in the use of vowels: e for ae or oe (as a result of a change in the pronunciation of diphthongs), sometimes i for e or e for i, sometimes u for o or o for u (similarity in the pronunciation of these vowels was influential here). I and y were also confused.
2.   D and t could be interchanged.
3.   In many authors, ci was written for ti, and probably pronounced tsi (cf. *oracio*, *nacio* and the Italian pronunciation of ci or ce); ti could be written for ci.
4.   Frequently, c was substituted for qu, and *vice versa*.
5.   An extra p could be inserted.
6.   F for ph was frequent.
7.   H could be inserted or omitted. Such variations in the use of h as *nichil* and *michi* may reflect a changing pronunciation, the palatalization of the h sound to a k sound.
8.   There can be confusion in ML in the use of simple or double consonants, e.g., *Bachus* for *Bacchus*.

Vocabulary.
1.   In ML words frequently developed somewhat different meanings from the ones they had in CL, e.g., *perfidus, comes, discretus, solacium, virtus*.
2.   In response to Christianity and the developing ecclesiastical liturgy and bureaucracy, new words were created, adapted from CL, or adopted from other languages (especially Greek, but also Hebrew), and from the Scriptures: e.g., *benedictio, abbas, dominus, oratio, pietas, episcopus, clerus, ecclesia*.

3. Many new ML words were created with suffixes such as *-amen, -anus, osus, -arius,* on the base of CL words.

4. Many new compounds were created, often but not always with the meaning of the simple form.

5. Diminutives were very frequent, often without special "diminutive" meaning.

Nouns.

1. The gender of nouns might be changed.

2. There was frequent confusion between the forms of 3rd and 5th declension nouns.

3. An abstract noun was often used for a concrete, e.g., *Graecia* for "Greeks."

4. The neuter plural of the adjective was frequently used substantively, often simply as a plural noun (as in CL) but also as a singular feminine abstract noun (e.g., *fortia,* "violence, power"); sometimes this distinction is hard to make, e.g., does *tetra noctis* mean "the horror of the night" or "the horrors of the night"?

Adjectives.

1. Many new compound adjectives arose in LL and ML, e.g., *florigerus.*

2. The comparative adjective or adverb was often used with positive or superlative force. The positive could sometimes have comparative force.

Cases.

1. Some authors were careless—or free—with the use of cases.

2. In ML, duration of time was often expressed by the ablative instead of the accusative.

3. The gerund in the ablative case often replaced the present participle in agreement with a noun or pronoun.

4. Prepositional phrases often replaced the use of cases alone (see below).

Pronouns. The clear distinction between the pronouns was lost in ML.

1. *Hic, iste* and *ille* were often used interchangeably.

2. *Ipse* might be used as a demonstrative pronoun, or might sometimes be simply superfluous.

3. *Sui, sibi, se, se* were not always reflexive and might be used for the oblique cases of *is.* The same was true of the reflexive adjective *suus.*

4. The personal pronoun was not necessarily emphatic; cf. the use of *il, elle,* in modern French.

Prepositions. In ML prepositions often developed unusual meanings and uses, and were often used where a case ending would be sufficient in CL. New prepositions were developed from adverbs, participles, and nouns.

1. *De* could indicate cause, material, a partitive idea, etc.; cf. *de* in modern French or Italian. It frequently thus replaced the genitive. *De* could also be used for *post* or *ex.*

2. *Cum* or *sub* could express means or instrument, though the ablative alone was also still used.
3. *Prae* could mean "because of"; it could follow a comparative, take an ablative, and mean "than."
4. *In* could mean "composed of, with, by means of."
(Certain writers were particularly unclassical in their use of prepositions; cf. Nos. 9, 29).

Tenses. Tenses could be used with more freedom than in CL, and on occasion even inaccurately.
1. The imperfect, perfect and pluperfect could be interchanged.
2. Present and future tenses could be confused.
3. There was often confusion with the verb forms in conditional sentences.
4. The frequent use of periphrastic tenses reflected the development towards the use of auxiliary verbs in Romance languages (e.g., *il est venu*); cf. No. 2.108: *audita est* for *auditur*; No. 12 s.12.3: *eris factura* ("you will do").
5. Compound tenses were frequently formed with *fui, fuissem*, etc., instead of *sum, essem*, etc.

Indirect Discourse. The accusative and infinitive of the CL indirect discourse construction were often replaced by a substantive clause introduced by *quod, quia, quoniam,* or *ut* ; both CL and ML forms of indirect discourse could appear in the same text.

Infinitive.
1. The infinitive (instead of the CL purpose clause with *ut* and the subjunctive) could be used to convey purpose.
2. It could be used with verbs that in CL would require a subjunctive.

Subjunctive. There were all kinds of variation in the uses of the subjunctive.
1. The sequence of tenses was frequently violated.
2. The distinction between indicative and subjunctive in subordinate clauses often broke down; for instance, an indicative could be used in an indirect question.
3. Subjunctives in conditional sentences were used in a variety of ways, e.g., the imperfect subjunctive in clauses of the future less vivid condition, or an imperfect instead of a pluperfect subjunctive in past contrary to fact conditions. Similarly, the tenses of potential subjunctives could be used in an unclassical way, e.g., an imperfect instead of a present subjunctive.
4. Tenses of the optative subjunctive might be confused, e.g., an imperfect subjunctive might be used in a possible wish (in CL, only in an unreal or impossible wish.)
5. Other conjunctions (especially *quod*) were used in place of *ut* in subjunctive clauses. (*Quod* became an all-purpose conjunction for "that".)

Medieval Verse Technique

There were two major techniques of versification in the Middle Ages. By the first, poets continued to write in the quantitative meters of the classical world, where the length of the syllable determined the metrical pattern. A variety of classical meters continued in use throughout the Middle Ages, though the hexameter and the pentameter were the most popular. During periods when the classics were most determinedly emulated (for instance, during the Carolingian period or during the twelfth century) and in the hands of highly learned poets, the medieval quantitative meters were almost indistinguishable from the ancient. For instance, even the end of line cadences of the best classical models were carefully imitated. A poet such as Hildebert aimed for the more regular Virgilian line endings such as - u u l - - or - u l u - -, while avoiding frequent use of polysyllabic or monosyllabic words at the end or endings such as ... - l u u l - -. Various licenses of prosody were allowed or taken, most notably in vowel quantity; such licenses differ in different periods of the Middle Ages. Some of these variations in quantity were not so much a matter of error as of changes in pronunciation, as for instance the pronunciation of ae as short e. Generally, hiatus was avoided; on the other hand, though elision was allowed as in the classical models by some poets, it was avoided by others.

At some point during the very early Middle Ages, for reasons about which scholars continue to disagree, there began to develop forms of rhythmic poetry. Here the metrical patterns were no longer based on the length of syllable but rather on the number of syllables and on word accent or stress. Account of the stress was usually taken at the part of the line before the caesura and at the line end; the stress could be paroxytone (*amáre*) or proparoxytone (*témpore*). Typical earlier examples of this type of poetry are the Merovingian fragment (No. 4 in this collection), where the line-end stress is paroxytone and the lines have seven or nine syllables, and the tenth century *Iam dulcis amica venito* (No. 12 in this collection), in which only the number of syllables in the line is fixed—and that number occasionally varies by one or two syllables. By the eleventh or twelfth centuries there regularly occur not only a fixed pattern of word accent at the caesurae or the ends of lines, but also a regular alteration of stressed and non-stressed syllables throughout the line (e.g., No. 18), and complex stanzaic forms appear (e.g., No. 27). Many scholars believe that these patterns of stress developed in imitation of quantitative meters; that is, poets tended to place word accent where there had been a long syllable in the quantitative meter. In considering stress in ML poetry, one should note: (1) "secondary stress" seems to fall on such syllables as the last syllable of a proparoxytone word or on the first syllable of a four syllable paroxytone word, and "metrical words"—word combinations usually including monosyllables or enclitic-type words, e.g. *folio-sum* in line 4 of No. 18—seem to help in creating the rhythmic patterns. (2) Further, the demand for "perfect pattern" of stress and non-stress (or of syllable counting) is largely a chimaera: medieval poets, like modern poets, were capable of varying the expected line pattern for special effects.

During the course of the Middle Ages the use of rhyme appeared in both quantitative and rhythmic verse. Assonance and rhyme were used by the classical poets for special effects but never in regular patterns. However, rhyme came to play an increasingly large role in many medieval poems. Originally, rhymes were used in a limited, repetitive, or sporadic fashion and were very simple: merely a correspondence of final vowel, final consonant, or of both final vowel and consonant. Though a fairly subtle use of rhyme appears in such early figures as Gottschalk or the Irish and Anglo-Saxon poets, "full" two-syllable rhymes employed in complex patterns throughout a poem only became common by the twelfth century. In quantitative poetry, the use of rhyme often fundamentally altered the sound of classical poetry. In lines such as

hora novissima, tempora pessima sunt, vigilemus.
ecce minaciter imminet arbiter ille supremus

the rhymes at caesurae and line ends coincide with the accent of the words, change the classical system of caesura pattern, and create in many ways a totally new kind of poetry. Pronunciation variations at different periods or in different areas influenced the nature of rhyme. For instance, all during the Middle Ages, both ae and oe were pronounced as e, and so rhyme with e; at certain periods, e and i rhyme, as do o and u.

A large portion of medieval poetry was written to be sung. The nature of its accompanying music must have influenced poetic form, but there are severe limitations to understanding medieval music, most notably the difficulty of understanding medieval musical notation. From the beginning, the two strands of medieval music, religious and secular, were intertwined and cross-fertilizing. Christian hymnody (descended from the Jewish liturgy of the Temple and then the synagogue, and well-established by the 4th century) and Gregorian chant clearly influenced secular song, both Latin and, later, vernacular. Secular melodies seem on occasion to have been borrowed for the new liturgical form of the ninth century, the sequence. Two major periods of poetic creativity were also periods of musical innovation: the ninth century, and the late eleventh through the early thirteenth century. For the ninth century only a few traces of secular music are left (see below on No. 6), but in religious music the Carolingian period gave birth to original forms of music inserted into the liturgy, the trope and the more important sequence. Poets and musicians were stimulated by the new meeting of Gallic and Roman culture or, in reaction to the unity of regular liturgical music (the Roman chant) imposed by Charlemagne, sought new outlets for their creativity. The early sequence (called "archaic") probably originated from the singing of a long series of notes (the *jubilus*) on the final a of the *Alleluia* of the gradual in the Mass. An early writer of sequences, Notker of St. Gall in Switzerland (*ca.* 884), tells us that it was very difficult to remember such complex, wordless melodies; he therefore decided to write words to fit the notes (one syllable per note) as an aid to memory. The early sequences thus are essentially prose, like some of the earliest Christian hymns, whose words and word order are determined by the melody. The *Alleluia* and the final *jubilus* seem to have been sung in alternation between a soloist and a choir or between two choirs; early sequences often have a pattern of strophe/antistrophe in which the stanza pairs are similar to each other in pattern of syllables but different from the other pairs; often there is a single introductory stanza and/or a single concluding stanza, presumably sung by all voices together. Strophe and antistrophe pairs often display extensive parallelism in words, syntax, and ideas. Though in origin (probably) a religious form and though performed as part of the Mass, some of the early sequence melodies seem to have been borrowed from secular songs, and the sequence structure was widely used for secular poetry (as in No. 11 below).

By the later eleventh century, much more secular music is recorded, increasingly written for vernacular as well as Latin verses. Popular musical forms, such as the use of refrains and dance music, influence even Latin lyric. Music was universal: the same melody was used for a Latin religious lyric as for a troubadour's song (see Philip the Chancellor, *Quisquis cordis et oculi*, Volume III No. 33); a Latin Christmas sequence was borrowed for an Anglo-Norman drinking song; the refrain of a French love song was used for a Latin rondeau *Veni, Sancte Spiritus*. The development of more complex music (polyphony in particular), faster tempo, and an increasing emphasis on the importance of music over text. parallels changes in rhythmic poetry: more complex stanza patterns, disyllabic rhyme, regular alternation of stressed and unstressed syllables, more emphasis overall on the aural quality of the words. Later sequences (the "regular" sequence) were influenced by the "new" rhythmic poetry and adopted the use of one recurrent stanza pattern, regular rhythm, and the use of rhyme; they kept only the special musical dimension of a changing melody for each new pair of stanzas. Another new musical form originating at the same time as the "regular" sequence was the *conductus*. This rhythmic song, with a complex melody, disyllabic rhyme and a single repeated (but complex) stanza form, was originally an accompaniment to religious processions and then adapted to a variety of religious uses; it was often polyphonic, it contained musical embellishments (*caudae*) at important points, and it was closely related to vernacular, troubadour lyric (cf. No. 33).

In order to describe the patterns of rhythmic poetry, the format of Dag Norberg (*Introduction à L'Étude de la Versification Latine Médiévale*, Stockholm, 1958) will be adapted.

1. Arabic numbers indicate the number of syllables per colon (the part of a line before a fixed caesura) or line.

2. A *p* for paroxytone or *pp* for proparoxytone following the arabic number will indicate the word accent of the last word in the colon or line. A $^{\circ}$ will indicate that there is no fixed end cadence. (There will be no attempt to indicate regularity of word accent within lines.)

3. If a poem has a stanza form, the lines will be linked by a +; the + is also used to link fixed cola within a line. Arabic numbers placed before x will indicate repeated line types in a stanza.

4. Rhyme is indicated by letters of the alphabet placed after the rhythmic indicators. If a rhyme is repeated in most or all of the stanzas of a poem, the letter will be capitalized. If there is no rhyme at the end of a line, an x is used. (Rhyme between caesura end and line end will not be indicated, nor will assonance patterns that are not true rhymes.)

5. *Refr.* (followed by rhythmic and rhyme indicators) will indicate a refrain. Rhyme schemes will be marked with reference to the first stanza, which they often imitate.

An example should make this method of notation clear. The Goliardic line (e.g., *Aestuans intrinsecus ira vehementi*; cf. No. 18 below) is described as 7pp + 6p, and, as this poem is bound into four-line stanzas by its rhyme scheme, the metrical pattern will be indicated as

$$4 \times (7pp + 6p) \,/\, aaaa.$$

(There is a fixed caesura after seven syllables, with the stress before the caesura being proparoxytone; six syllables follow the caesura, with a paroxytone word at the end of the line. All four line-ends rhyme but there is no rhyme before the caesura.)

Bibliography
(Works Often Cited)

Adcock	F. Adcock, tr., *The Virgin and the Nightingale*, Newcastle upon Tyne, 1983.
A & G	J. B. Greenough *et al.*, eds., *Allen and Greenough's New Latin Grammar for Schools and Colleges*, Boston, 1903.
Anal. hymn.	*Analecta Hymnica Medii Aevi*, ed., G.M. Dreves, C. Blume, and H.M. Bannister, 55 vols., 1886-1922.
CB	*Carmina Burana*, ed. by A. Hilka, O. Schumann, B. Bischoff, Heidelberg, 1930-
Curtius	E.R.Curtius, *European Literature and the Latin Middle Ages*, New York, 1953.
Dronke, *ML*	P. Dronke, *The Medieval Lyric*, 2nd. ed., Cambridge, 1977.
Dronke, *MLREL*	P. Dronke, *Medieval Latin and the Rise of European Love Lyric*, Oxford, 1968.
Gedichte	K. Strecker, ed., *Moralisch-satirische Gedichte Walters von Châtillon*, Heidelberg, 1929.
Godman	P. Godman, *Poetry of the Carolingian Renaissance*, London, Duckworth, 1985.
Lieder	K. Strecker, ed., *Die Lieder Walters von Châtillon in der Handschrift 351 von St. Omer*, Berlin, 1925.
MLLM	J.F. Niermeyer, *Mediae Latinitatis Lexicon Minus*, Leiden, 1976.
Norberg, *Introduction*	D. Norberg, *Introduction à L'Étude de la Versification Latine Médiévale*, Stockholm, 1958.
Norberg, *Manuel*	D. Norberg, *Manuel Pratique de Latin Médiéval*, Paris, 1980.
OBMLV	F. J. E. Raby, ed., *Oxford Book of Medieval Latin Verse*, Oxford, 1959.
OLD	P.G.W. Glare, *Oxford Latin Dictionary*, Oxford, 1982.
Parlett	D. Parlett, *Selections from the Carmina Burana: a New Verse Translation*, Penguin, 1986.
Raby, *SLP*	F.J.E. Raby, *Secular Latin Poetry*, 2nd ed., Oxford, 1957.
Walsh	P.G. Walsh, *Thirty Poems from the Carmina Burana*, Reading, 1976.
Watenphul and Krefeld	H. Watenphul and H. Krefeld, *Die Gedichte des Archipoeta*, Heidelberg, 1958.
Wilhelm	J. J. Wilhelm, *The Cruelest Month: Spring, Nature and Love in Classical and Medieval Lyrics*, New Haven, Yale University Press, 1965.

No. 1
Venantius Fortunatus: Si nequeo praesens

Si nequeo praesens, absens tibi solvo tributum,
    ut probet affectum, mater amata, meum.
Si non essem [absens], facerem quodcumque iuberes:
    obsequiis parvis forte placeret iners;
pectore devoto set rustica lingua dedisset   5
    pastoris calamo matris in aure sonum;
imperiis famulans tererem mea membra diurnis,
    servirent dominae subdita colla suae;
nulla recusarent digiti, puteoque profundo
    quae manus hoc scripsit prompta levaret aquas,   10
protraheret vites et surcula figeret hortis,
    plantaret, coleret dulce libenter holus.
Splendor erat tecum mea membra ardere coquina
    et nigra de puro vasa lavare lacu.
Hinc tibi nunc absens Marcelli munera misi,   15
    cui dedit excelsum vita beata locum,
et si displiceant indigno verba relatu,
    complaceant animo signa superna tuo.
Sis longaeva mihi cum nata et messe sororum,
    virgineoque choro crescat ovile dei.   20
Si tua verba dares, essent plus dulcia quam si
    floribus electis mella dedisset apes.

Commentary

Venantius Fortunatus (c. 540 - c. 600 A.D.), born and classically educated in north Italy, spent his adult life in what is now France, winning patronage and friendship by his writing of verses for important persons at court and for prominent clergy. This was a period of political and military turmoil among the descendants of Clovis, and one of cultural transition in which the Gallo-Romans were clinging to their classical traditions and the Franks were eagerly trying to assimilate the presitigious Roman culture. As the only major Latin poet of the last part of the sixth century, Fortunatus played a key role. He very skillfully adapted the conventions of classical panegyric to suit his Merovingian audience; like the best of the classical encomiasts, Venantius created idealized images of kingship that were meant to inspire and admonish, as well as flatter, the recipients (Godman, *Poets and Emperors, passim*). His success was noteworthy: he ended as bishop of Poitiers (from 591 until his death) and was later sedulously imitated by poets of the Carolingian era.

From 567 he was settled in Poitiers as versifier, friend, and advisor to Radegunde. This remarkable woman, daughter of the king of Thuringia, had been captured at the age of twelve by the Franks and at eighteen married to

King Clotaire (Lothar), son of Clovis. Gregory of Tours describes the history of this "trophy wife" as follows: "When the time came to return home Lothar took with him as his share of the booty Radegund, the daughter of King Berthar. Later he married her. This did not stop him afterwards from arranging for her brother to be murdered by assassins. Radegund turned to God, took the habit of a religious and built a nunnery for herself in Poitiers. She was famous for her prayers, her vigils and her charities, and she became so well known that the common people looked upon her as a saint" (*The History of the Franks* 3.7; cf. *The Oxford Dictionary of Saints*).

Fortunatus' most famous works are the two distinguished hymns *Pange lingua gloriosi* and *Vexilla regis prodeunt*, but a number of verses from his *Carmina* (a collection of brief poems on various subjects, often in the form of letters to friends) give a detailed picture of the unusual relationship between himself, Radegunde, and Agnes, Radegunde's protégée and the abbess of the monastery of the Holy Cross that Radegunde had founded at Poitiers. Fortunatus' portrayal of his affectionate friendship with his "mother" Radegunde and her "daughter" Agnes has a distinctive intimacy and humor.

Ms.: The poems of Leo's appendix, in which *Si nequeo praesens* is found, are taken from Paris MS. lat. 13048. This is a ninth century ms., a collection of miscellaneous works (e.g., of Cassiodorus and St. Augustine); Fortunatus' poems are on f. 31-58. In Leo's edition of Fortunatus, the poems for Radegunde and Agnes are to be found in books 8, 11 and the appendix; only the poems of book 8 were published by Fortunatus, the rest being apparently collected by his friends after his death and perhaps not originally intended for publication.

Meter: Quantitative; elegiacs. With elision and generally correct syllabic quantities (but cf. *solvo,* where the final o is shortened for metrical convenience). Both hexameter and pentameter lines are in accordance with regular classical line structures. No regular rhyme, though Fortunatus, like the Augustan elegists, fairly frequently rhymes the two halves of his pentameters, cf. lines 2, 8, 16, 18.

Bibliography: Dronke, *MLREL,* v.1, pp. 200-209; Venantius Fortunatus, *Opera Poetica,* F. Leo, ed., *Monumenta Germaniae Historica: Auctores Antiquissimi* 4, 1881, Appendix no. 22, pp. 286-7; J.W. George, *Venantius Fortunatus: a Latin Poet in Merovingian Gaul,* Oxford, 1992; P. Godman, *Poets and Emperors: Frankish Politics and Carolingian Poetry,* Oxford, 1987, pp. 1-37; B. J. Rogers, *The Poems of Venantius Fortunatus,* Ann Arbor, Michigan (University Microfilms), 1970; Raby, *SLP,* v.1, pp. 127-142.

1 **nequeo:** "be unable."
   solvo tributum: CL "pay a tax"; here, "offer a tribute."
2 **probet:** "win approval for, prove"; its subject is *tributum* from the previous line.

	mater: Fortunatus frequently calls Radegunde *mater,* cf. 9.4, App. 24, App. 29.
3	**essem ... facerem:** contrary to fact condition.
	[absens]: added by Guérard, an early editor (*Notices et Extraits,* XII, 1831, part. II, p. 75 ff.). If this is the correct text, Fortunatus is stressing the vital situation underlying the poem, separation from Radegunde, cf. *absens* in lines 1, 3, 15.
	iuberes: subjunctive in a relative clause of characteristic.
4	**obsequiis:** "services."
	placeret ... iners: "a clumsy man might please ... "; the subjunctives in this and the following lines are potential rather than contrary to fact.
5	**set:** variant for *sed.* Contrasts *rustica* with the ablative of description *pectore devoto* :"devoted though inelegant."
6	**pastoris calamo:** "shepherd's pipe," a deprecatory reference to the poet's *rustica lingua.*
	in aure: for CL *in aurem* to express the idea of motion towards or into; cf. *Linguistic Note* (Cases 1).
7	**famulans:** < *famulor,* "serve."
	tererem: here, "wear out."
8	**dominae:** dative with *servirent.*
	subdita: "subject, subservient" (perfect passive participle of *subdo*).
	colla: poetic plural.
9	**nulla:** object of *recusarent*; "nothing, no tasks."
10	**manus:** subject of *levaret,* appearing within the relative clause *quae ... scripsit* of which it is technically the antecedent.
	prompta: "promptly, eagerly," adjective modifying *manus,* best translated as adverb.
11	**protraheret ... hortis:** Rogers suggests this refers to the rooting of the tips of vines in the soil.
	surcula: < CL *surculus,* "twig used in grafting or other form of propagation"; cf. *Linguistic Note* (Nouns 1).
12	**plantaret, coleret:** asyndeton, common in Fortunatus' poetry.
	holus: neut. sing., "vegetables," here probably "garden," modified by *dulce.* Cf. *Linguistic Note* (Vocabulary 1).
13-14.	**Splendor ... lacu:** Radegunde, though once queen, declined to be head of the monastery she founded and apparently chose to perform the most menial duties there.
13	**Splendor:** here, "glory"; but also an example of the light imagery Fortunatus favors (Dronke, *MLREL,* v.1, p. 201).
	erat: The imperfect indicative is used place of the subjunctive, as often in phrases denoting necessity, propriety or desirability (*splendor erat*).
	coquina: CL "art of cooking"; ML "kitchen"; the preposition *in* usually required with the ablative of place where is omitted by poetic license.

14   **lacu:** CL "lake, pool"; here, probably "water." See on *holus* 12.

15   **Marcelli munera:** "gift of St. Marcellus' life" (Rogers). This poem was apparently sent to Radegunde to accompany a life of St. Marcellus, perhaps in verse like Fortunatus' still extant life of St. Martin. Marcellus was a noted bishop of Paris in the early 5th century, protecting his flock against invaders and working many miracles, including killing a dragon; Fortunatus is said to have had to rely on vague, oral tradition in composing his now lost *Vita* of Marcellus.

16   **excelsum:** "lofty, noble"; the reference is presumably to paradise.
     beata: "happy, fortunate," perhaps "blessed" (because of his piety). Both *excelsum* and *beata* recall biblical language, e.g., *Matt.* 5.3 ff., *Luc.*2.14.

17-18   **displiceant ... complaceant:** future less vivid condition.

17   **relatu:** "narration, style"; an ablative of cause.

18   **signa:** "miracles."
     superna: CL "celestial"; here, presumably "saintly."

19-20   **Sis ... crescat:** optative subjunctive, used to express a wish. Fortunatus' poems, as is natural considering their often epistolary nature, frequently end with good wishes for the recipient (e.g., 8.6, 8.9, App. 21).

19   **mihi:** ethical dative, indicating the interest felt by the speaker in the idea being expressed.
     nata: Agnes, whom Venantius often calls Radegunde's daughter in his imaginary family where Radegunde is mother and Agnes is her daughter and his sister.
     messe sororum: "harvest of nuns." Rogers, *passim*, calls attention to Fortunatus' extensive use of nature imagery (cf. 2.1, 8.7), where spring bringing the rebirth of nature mirrors Christ's resurrection and his fructifying power; in this poem the imagery is specifically agricultural, cf. 11-12, 20-22.

20   **choro:** here, "band, company" (an emendation by Guérard of the ms. *thoro*); ablative of material, in poetry often used without a preposition.
     crescat: "flourish."
     ovile: "sheep-fold."

21   **verba dares:** Fortunatus is requesting an answer from Radegunde to his poetic letter; Radegunde at times apparently wrote verses in answer to his (Dronke, *MLREL*, v.1, p. 203). Godman (*Poets and Emperors*, pp. 15 ff.) notes that Venantius frequently praises his patrons' *dulcedo* ("sweetness," of conversation and of food given to the needy); this *dulcedo*, specially characteristic of the sweetness of language, redounds to his own credit, since he is the writer of sweet verses.
     dares ... essent: a future less vivid condition; see *Linguistic Note* (Subjunctive 3).

plus dulcia: a ML variant for CL *dulciora*.

22   **electis:** "choice" (perfect passive participle of *eligo*).

mella: poetic plural < *mel*, "honey."

apes: nominative singular; see *Linguistic Note* (Nouns 2).

No. 2
Columbanus: Mundus iste transibit

Mundus iste transibit,
cottidie decrescit;
nemo vivens manebit,
nullus vivus remansit.

Totum humanum genus   5
ortu utitur pari,
et de simili vita
fine cadit aequali;

differentibus vitam
mors incerta subripit,   10
omnes superbos vagos
meror mortis corripit.

Quod pro Christo largiri
nolunt, omnes avari
inoportune amittunt;   15
post se colligunt alii.

Parvum ipsi viventes
deo dare vix audent;
morti cuncta relinquunt,
nihil de ipsis habent.   20

Cottidie decrescit
vita praesens quam amant;
indeficiens manebit
sibi poena quam parant.

Lubricum quod labitur   25
conantur colligere,
et hoc quod se seducit
minus timent credere.

Dilexerunt tenebras
tetras magis quam lucem.   30
Imitari contemnunt
vitae Dominum ducem.

Velut in somnis regnant;
una hora laetantur,
sed aeterna tormenta   35
adhuc illis parantur.

Caeci nequaquam vident
quid post obitum restat,
peccatoribus impiis
quod impietas praestat.   40

Cogitare convenit
te haec cuncta, amice.
Absit tibi amare
huius formulam vitae.

Omnis en caro foenum   45
flagrans, licet florida,
sicque quasi flos foeni
omnis eius est gloria;

orto sole arescit
foenum et flos deperit;   50
sic est omnis iuventus,
virtus cum defecerit.

Pulchritudo hominum
senescens delabitur.
Omnis decor pristinus   55
cum dolore eraditur.

Vultus Christi radius
prae cunctis amabilis
magis diligendus est
quam flos carnis fragilis.   60

Caveto, filiole,
feminarum species,
per quas mors ingreditur,
non parva pernicies.

Plerique perpessi sunt   65
poenarum incendia,
voluntatis lubricae
nolentes dispendia.

Poculum impiisimae
noli umquam bibere;   70
inde multos plerumque
vides laetos ridere;

nam quoscumque videris
ridere inaniter,
scito in novissimis   75
quod flebunt amariter.

Conspice, carissime,
sic esse libidinem
ut morsum mortiferum,
quod vincit dulcedinem.   80

Noli pronus pergere
per viam mortalium,
qua multis evenisse
conspicis naufragium.

Perge inter laqueos   85
cum suspensis pedibus,
per quos captos ceteros
incautos conperimus.

De terrenis eleva
tui cordis oculos;   90
ama amantissimos
angelorum populos;

beata familia,
quae in altis habitat,
ubi senex non gemat,   95
neque infans vagiat,

ubi laudis Domini
nulla vox retinetur,
ubi non esuritur,
ubi numquam sititur,   100

ubi cibo superno
plebs caelestis pascitur,
ubi nemo moritur
quia nemo nascitur,

ubi aula regia   105
... ...
in qua male resonans
nulla vox audita est,

ubi vita viridis
veraque futura est,   110
quam nec mors nec meroris
metus consumpturus est.

Laeti leto transacto
laetum regem videbunt;
cum regnante regnabunt,   115
cum gaudente gaudebunt.

Tunc dolor, tunc taedium,
tunc labor delebitur,
tunc rex regum, rex mundus
a mundis videbitur.   120

Commentary

This song, in the form of advice to a friend or student, was probably written by Saint Columbanus (*ca.* 543-615). A member of the monastic order at Bangor in Ireland and teacher there for many years, Columbanus spent the latter part of his life spreading the influence of Irish monasticism in France (Luxeuil), Switzerland (S. Gall), and Italy (Bobbio). Outspoken, ascetic, and idealistic, Columbanus exerted a reforming influence on the French church and monasticism and permanently affected the medieval church with his ideas of private confession and penance and of monastic independence from diocesan control. Columbanus' works include letters, sermons, the earliest surviving Irish monastic Rule, and poems. The poem printed here reflects Columbanus' extensive knowledge of the classics and is representative of the ideas and phraseology of the saint's other writings (cf. *Epistle* 5, *Sermones* 3 and 5, the verses to Hunaldus, Sethus, and Fidolius); it expatiates upon the favorite medieval contrast between the transitory and potentially sinful nature of this "life" (whose temptations can lead to eternal damnation) and the true "life" of Christian faith and, eventually, of paradise. There has been doubt of the authorship of the song, but Walker and others have argued that it is most probably by Columbanus.

Ms.: There are only two manuscript sources: the first a ms., Z, from Zurich (Zurich Stadtbibliothek C 78 (451) [s.IX/X], foll. 159-60 v) which originally contained no author's name but has a marginal addition of Columbanus' name by a later hand; the second, Siii, a ms. from St. Gall cited by Melchior Goldast (*Paraeneticorum Veterum,* Pars I, 1604, p. 153) but now lost.

Meter: This is an early example of rhythmic verse: 4 x (7º) / xaxa. (In two cases editors have emended the mss. to achieve an absolutely uniform seven syllable line pattern; this seems too rigid a standard for the rhythmic poetry of this period.) Columbanus seems to aim for two-syllable rhyme; however, many of the rhymes are less than perfect, though in some instances (e.g., 42, 44; 98, 100) this can be explained by differences of pronunciation. There is no elision (unless possibly in 15 and 56) and little concern for hiatus. There seem to be 2 instances of synizesis (*indeficiens* 23; *gloria* 48) and 3 instances of -ii counted as a single long -i sound (16, 39, 69), although this may be rather a matter of flexibility in the number of syllables per line.

    Bibliography: F.J.E. Raby, *Christian Latin Poetry*, 2nd ed., 1953, pp. 138-40; Walker, G.S.M. (ed.), *Sancti Columbani Opera*, (Scriptores Latini Hiberniae, v. 2), Dublin, 1957.

1	**mundus ... transibit:** The transitoriness of this life is a favorite theme of Columbanus: cf. *ad Hunaldum* 5, 15 (*Molles inlecebras vitae nunc sperne caducae; Lubrica mortalis cito transit gloria vitae*); *ad Sethum* 59-60; *Fidolio fratri suo* 106-109. **iste:** See *Linguistic Note* (Pronouns 1).
2	**decrescit:** "weakens, fades"; perhaps the imagery is of the waning moon, cf. *ortu* 6.
3-4	**nemo ... remansit:** Columbanus makes frequent use of plays on words: puns (cf. *mundus* 1 and 119-120, *laeti leto* 113); variations of grammatical form (as here, also 115-6); combinations of cognates (cf. 91); repetition (cf. 119); sound similarities (e.g., *lubricum ... labitur* 25, *flagrans ... florida* 46). With these techniques, Columbanus underlines the recurrent themes of his song.
6	**ortu:** "rising (of a heavenly body), birth, origin" (cf. on 2).
7-8	**de ... cadit:** "falls down from, sets from," in contrast to the imagery of *ortu ... pari*, 6.
9	**differentibus:** "postpone"; dative with *subripit*; its object is *vitam*. There is ambiguity in the meaning of *vita* throughout this poem: here, the true life of Christian faith and piety is intended (cf. 109-110); elsewhere the life of the fleshly and insubstantial world (e.g., 22, 44) is indicated.
10	**subripit:** for *subrepit*, "creep upon, insinuate into"; see *Linguistic Note* (Orthography 1).
11	**vagos:** "wandering," used of the heavenly bodies, especially the planets (as opposed to the fixed stars), *OLD* 1; also, "inconstant."
12	**meror:** CL *maeror*, "grief"; cf. *Linguistic Note* (Orthography 1).
13	**largiri:** "give generously, bestow."
15	**inoportune:** "inappropriately, unseasonably." Editors have emended, probably incorrectly, to the more usual spelling *inportune* to preserve the meter; cf. **Meter** above.
16	**se:** See *Linguistic Note* (Pronouns 3); cf. *sibi*, 24 and *se*, 27.
17	**parvum:** adverbial accusative with *viventes*.
20	**de ipsis:** This phrase probably represents a CL dative of reference, *sibi*.
21-24	**cottidie ... parant:** use of parallel phrasing to emphasize contrasting ideas.

21   **decrescit:** cf. 2; an example of Columbanus' extensive use of repetitions throughout this poem.

23   **indeficiens:** "unfailing, that never stops"; from LL. Cf. *deficio*, "fail, die, wane (of the moon)."

25   Cf. Ovid *Fast.* 5.476: *lubrica prensantes effugit umbra manus* (of the ghost of Remus slipping from the embrace of his family).
    lubricum: object of *colligere*, 26; in ML adjectives were often used in place of nouns; see below *terrenis* 89, *altis* 94. See also on 3-4.

27   **hoc:** object of *credere* ("believe as true, accept the reality of," *OLD* 5, with the accusative) and antecedent of *quod*.

28   **minus:** used as a negative with *timere*, "do not adequately fear."

29-30   Cf. *John* 3.19: *dilexerunt homines magis tenebras quam lucem*.
    tetras: CL *taeter*, "vile, horrible" (not in the Biblical passage).

34   **una hora:** Cf. *Linguistic Note* (Cases 2).

36   **adhuc:** "already."

37   **nequaquam:** "by no means, not at all."

38-40   **quid ... quod:** Columbanus switches from an indirect question (without a subjunctive; cf. *Linguistic Note*, Subjunctive 2) to a relative clause whose antecedent is the indirect question *quid ... restat*.

39   **peccatoribus impiis:** dative with *praestat* ("offers, furnishes"), 40.

42   **amice:** This begins a series of vocatives (61,77) and commands (43, 61, 70, etc.) that represent Columbanus' advice to the friend or student he is addressing; this form, the giving of advice, is present in four of Columbanus' five extant poems.

43   **absit:** hortatory subjunctive; its subject is the infinitive phrase *amare ... vitae*.

44   **formulam:** "shape, pattern, type"; perhaps thought of here as a true diminutive of *forma*, "outward appearance (as distinguished from substance, reality)," *OLD*. Cf. *species*, 62.

45-50   **omnis ... deperit:** Cf. *Isaiah* 40.6: *omnis caro faenum et omnis gloria eius quasi flos agri. exsiccatum est faenum et cedidit flos; Letter to Jacob* 1.10-11: *dives autem in humilitate sua quoniam sicut flos faeni transibit. exortus est enim sol cum ardore et arefecit faenum. et flos eius decidit. et decor vultus eius deperiit.*

45   **foenum:** "grass."

46   **flagrans:** perhaps "(easily) burning," < *flagro*, "burn", "burn (with passion)." *Flagro* could be confused with *fragro* or *fraglo*, "smell (sweet)"; this would be an attractive interpretation here except that *licet* ("although") *florida* follows.

47   **sic ... quasi:** "just as, like."

48   **eius:** refers to *caro*, 45.

49   **orto sole:** ablative absolute; cf. 6.

52   **virtus:** "strength, vigor," but also "moral excellence."
    defecerit: "has failed"; cf. *indeficiens*, 23.

55	**pristinus:** "former."
	cum dolore: See *Linguistic Note* (Prepositions 2).
56	**eraditur:** "scrape away, erase"; editors have emended to *raditur* to preserve the meter.
57	**radius:** here probably, "light"; in apposition to *vultus*; possibly used in confusion for *radians*, < *radio*, "shine." There may be a pun (or a contamination) with *eraditur*, 56.
58	**prae cunctis:** This phrase can be understood as "before all" or *amabilis* can be interpreted as *amabilior* followed by the ablative with *prae*, as often in ML.
59	**diligendus:** "to be loved."
61	**caveto:** the future imperative, in CL used where there is a specific reference to future time. See *Linguistic Note* (Tenses 2).
	filiole: vocative of *filiolus*, "little son"; see *Linguistic Note* (Vocabulary 5).
65	**perpessi sunt:** < *perpetior*, "experience to the full."
66	**voluntatis lubricae:** Cf. 25.
68	**dispendia:** < *dispendium*, "loss" (perhaps a poetic plural); in the plural, this word can refer to the losses or decreases of the waning moon.
69	**impiissimae:** sc. *voluntatis;* genitive dependent on *poculum.*
70	**noli ... bibere:** "don't drink"; negative imperative.
71	**inde:** "from that."
73	**videris:** future perfect.
75	**scito:** See above on 61.
	in novissimis: "at the last, in the last (days)."
76	**quod flebunt:** See *Linguistic Note* (Indirect discourse).
78-79	**sic ... ut:** See above on 47.
79	**morsum mortiferum:** "deadly bite"; the reference is to Adam's eating the forbidden fruit.
81	**noli ... pergere:** See above on 70.
	pronus: "headlong"; the reference is primarily to the posture of a person plunging down a road (*pronus* modifies the understood subject) but secondarily perhaps to the downward slope of the road itself.
83	**qua:** "by which, on which."
	multis: dative with *evenisse* ("happen to").
84	**naufragium:** "shipwreck." The accusative subject of *evenisse* in indirect discourse after *conspicis.*
86	**suspensis pedibus:** "with hesitant feet" (Walker), or perhaps "with lightly-stepping feet" or "on tiptoe."
87	**per quos:** The antecedent is *laqueos* ("snares"), 85.
	captos: for the perfect passive infinitive, *captos esse*, in indirect discourse after *conperimus* (< *comperio*, "learn") with *ceteros incautos* as its subject.
89	**terrenis:** "earthly things."

95-6   **gemat ... vagiat:** See *Linguistic Note* (Subjunctive 2). Columbanus may have used a subjunctive here because of the indefinite or generalizing idea, but he returns to the indicative with *retinetur* ("is restrained"), *esuritur*, etc.

99-100   **esuritur ... sititur:** This is the impersonal use of the passive, e.g., "there is (no) hunger, (no one) is hungry."

101   **cibo superno:** "celestial food," ablative with *pascor* ("feed on"), here deponent.

106   The mss. incorrectly repeat a part of line 102 here; Blume (*Analecta Hymnica*, 51, p. 353) conjectures *dulci cantu plena est.*

107   **male resonans:** "poorly resounding."

108   **audita est:** In CL this would be expressed as *auditur*; see *Linguistic Note* (Tenses 4).

109-10   **vita ... vera:** See above on 9.

110   **futura est:** See on 108 above.

111   **meroris:** See above on 12.

113   **leto transacto:** ablative absolute; *transacto* (< *transigo*): "passed, completed."

115-6   **regnante ... gaudente:** Participles (like adjectives, see above on 25) are often used as nouns in ML.

117   **taedium:** "weariness," or perhaps, with the ML meaning, "sorrow, mourning."

118   **delebitur:** < *deleo*, "destroy, abolish."

No. 3
Eugenius of Toledo: Vox philomela

Vox, philomela, tua cantus edicere cogit,
    inde tui laudem rustica lingua canit.
Vox, philomela, tua citharas in carmine vincit
    et superat miris musica flabra modis.
Vox, philomela, tua curarum semina pellit,   5
    recreat et blandis anxia corda sonis.
Florea rura colis, herboso caespite gaudes,
    frondibus arboreis pignera parva foves.
Cantibus ecce tuis recrepant arbusta canoris,
    consonat ipsa suis frondea silva comis.   10
Iudice me cygnus et garrula cedat hirundo,
    cedat et inlustri psittacus ore tibi.
Nulla tuos umquam cantus imitabitur ales,
    murmure namque tuo dulcia mella fluunt.
Dic ergo tremulos lingua vibrante susurros   15
    et suavi liquidum gutture pange melos.
Porrige dulcisonas attentis auribus escas;
    nolo tacere velis, nolo tacere velis.
Gloria summa tibi, laus et benedictio, Christe,
    qui praestas famulis haec bona grata tuis.   20

Commentary

    Eugenius of Toledo (d. 658), well-educated in the classics, a monk of Visigothic family and finally archbishop of Toledo (646-658), was the best of the Spanish poets of this period, writing a number of poems on moral, religious, and personal subjects, in differing quantitative meters. His poetry was very influential on writers of the Carolingian Renaissance. The poem printed here takes the nightingale, well-known classical symbol of love, grief, and loss derived from the various versions of the Greek myth of Procne and Philomela (Homer *Od.* 19.518-24; Ovid *Meta.* 6.424 ff.) and gives it a Christian significance (below, 19-20). The nightingale recurs in medieval poetry as happy spring bird that implies love (e.g., No. 12 below), as ambiguous symbol of love and grief (e.g., *Axe Phebus aureo, CB*, No. 44), and as Christian symbol of the soul contemplating Christ (e.g., John Pecham, *Philomena praevia temporis amoeni, OBMLV* #273).

    Ms.: The only ms. of importance for establishing the text of *Vox philomela* is a tenth century ms. in Visigothic letters (now the Codex Matritensis bibl. nat. 14,22, in Madrid); this ms. was once owned by Michael Ruyzius Azagra and then transferred to the library of Toledo cathedral. *Vox philomela* also appears, together with three other short epigrams about nightingales also by Eugenius, in three other mss. of the tenth - eleventh centuries (now in Paris, Brussels, and Bern).

Meter: Quantitative; elegiacs. Generally correct syllabic quantities, except that Eugenius, in company with many medieval poets, often lengthens the short vowel of a final syllable when it receives the ictus of the verse (i.e., the metrical stress), especially when such a syllable falls at a caesura (1, 3, 5, 7, 11). Both hexameter and pentameter lines are in accordance with regular classical line structures. Eugenius appears to be making some use of one-syllable rhyme or assonance between words at the caesura and end of a line (e.g., 4, 6, 7). (In this analysis, e and i, o and u, are considered to rhyme, as often in late antiquity and in the early Middle Ages.) No elision; no hiatus.

Bibliography: Adcock, pp. 18-19; Eugenii Toletani Episcopi, *Carmina*, ed. F. Vollmer, *MGH, Auct. Antiq.*, v. 14, pp. 231 ff. (*Vox philomela*, no. 33, p. 254); Godman, p. 20; *OBMLV* #62; Raby, "Philomena praevia temporis amoeni," *Melanges Joseph de Ghellinck*, Gembloux, 1951, v. 2 , pp. 435-48; W. Pfeffer, *The Change of Philomel: The Nightingale in Medieval Literature*, New York, 1985; Raby, *SLP*, v. 1, pp. 149 ff.; Wilhelm, pp. 79 ff. and *passim*.

1   **philomela:** Of the two etymologies (*philos*, "friend," plus *melos*, "song," and *philos* plus *melas*, "dark"), the positive meaning, "lover of song," is chosen here, as often in the Middle Ages, while the meaning of "friend of darkness" is less usual; but cf. Eugenius, *MGH*, no. 30, p. 253 (of the nightingale): *Sum noctis socia, sum cantus dulcis amica,/ nomen ab ambiguo sic philomela gero* (Wilhelm, p. 79, n. 19).
     tua: Note the lengthening of the final short vowel under the ictus (cf. above, **Meter**).
     cantus: fourth declension accusative plural, "songs" (used of both poetry and bird song).
     edicere: "utter the words of (a song)"; understand, as subject of this infinitive, either *me* or *poetam*.
2   **inde:** "therefore, so."
     tui: "of you"; objective genitive < *tu*.
     rustica lingua: "my pastoral muse."
3   **citharas:** "lyres."
4   **miris ... modis:** "in a remarkable manner, amazingly."
     musica flabra: "tuneful blasts," i.e., the music of wind instruments.
6   **et:** postponed, as often in poetry; grammatically, it should preceed *recreat*.
7   **caespite:** < *caespes*, "turf, soil,"; ablative with *gaudes*.
8   **pignera:** < *pignus*, "pledge," here, "offspring, children."
9   Cf. Virg. *Georgics* 2.328: *avia tum resonant avibus virgulta canoris*.
     recrepant: "ring, resound."
10   **consonat:** "re-echo (you), sound along with (you)."
     comis: < *coma*, "hair, foliage."

11   **iudice me:** ablative absolute, "if I were judge, according to my opinon."

         cedat: either iussive subjunctive, "let ... yield," or potential subjunctive, "would (probably) yield."

12   **et:** See above on 6.

         inlustri ... ore: ablative of description modifying *psittacus*, either (1) "with brilliant head" or (2) "with his clear voice"; the ambiguity is probably deliberate. *Inlustri* stands for *illustri*.

14   **murmure ... tuo:** "in your (soft) song"; in prose the preposition *in* would be required here.

         namque: postponed; see above on 6.

         mella: poetic plural < *mel*, "honey."

15   **susurros:** "whisperings, gentle sounds."

16   **liquidum:** "clear, melodious."

         gutture: < *guttur*, "throat."

         pange: "sing."

         melos: neuter accusative, "song."

17   **dulcisonas:** LL, "sweet-sounding"; see *Linguistic Note* (Adjectives 1).

         escas: "food."

18   This repetition in the two halves of the pentameter is similar to the technique of epanalepsis: the repetition, in elegiacs, of the first part of the hexameter in the second part of the pentameter.

         velis: subjunctive with *nolo*; *ut*, as often, is omitted.

19   The concluding two lines of this poem present interesting problems of interpretation.

         benedictio: "blessing" (from LL); see *Linguistic Note* (Vocabulary 2). (The final o is shortened, as frequently in ML.)

20   **haec bona grata:** "these pleasant good things."

No. 4
Dum ivi ambolare

Dum ivi ambolare
et bene cogetare
audivi avem adcladtire,
et cessed myhy inde
dolere, suspi[rare].   5

Commentary

This is a fragment of an early medieval song that has been preserved because it was written in the margin of a religious manuscript, the Lyon Psalter (Cod. Lugdunensis 425, once 351, f. 71v). The song appears to be a very early example of medieval secular rhythmic poetry. The handwriting, according to Peter Dronke, is of the Merovingian period.

Meter: Rhythmic. Lines 1, 2, 4 have 7 syllables, line 3 has 9. All the lines still extant are paroxytone and end with assonance in e.

Bibliography: Dronke, *MLREL*, v. 1, p. 220; *Poetae Latini Aevi Carolini* (Monumenta Germaniae Historica, 1881 ff.), v. 4.2, No. 91, p.652.

1   **ivi:** This is Vollmer's conjecture (cited in *Poetae Latini Aevi Carolini*), adopted by Dronke. The ms. has *myhy* (= *mihi*). If correct, *ivi ambolare ... cogetare* would represent periphrastic tenses such as English "I was walking" or Italian "*stavo parlando.*" See *Linguistic Note* (Tenses 4).
      ambolare: CL *ambulare*. This fragment as printed contains many examples of Merovingian spelling and, presumably, pronunciation. See *Linguistic Note* (Orthography) and below *cogetare* 2, *cessed*, *myhy* 4.

2   **cogetare:** CL *cogitare*.
3   **adcladtire:** "chattering" (Dronke); this appears to be a version of the verb *glattire* used by Suetonius (fr. 161, p. 250 Reiffersch) for the voices of puppies.
4   **cessed:** CL *cessit*. The subject is the infinitive *dolere* and probably the infinitive *suspirare* (see below).
      myhy: CL *mihi* (dative of reference).
      inde: "then."
5   **suspi[rare]:** "to sigh" (frequently a sign of lovesickness or passion, e.g., Horace *Carm.* 3.7.10). This is Dronke's conjecture for the ms. reading, given as *suspin ...* in *Poetae Latini Aevi Carolini*.

No. 5
Alcuin: Conveniunt subito cuncti

Conveniunt subito cuncti de montibus altis
pastores pecudum vernali luce sub umbra
arborea, pariter laetas celebrare Camenas;
adfuit et iuvenis Dafnis seniorque Palemon.
Omnes hi cuculo laudes cantare parabant.   5
Ver quoque florigero succinctus stemmate venit,
frigida venit Hiems, rigidis hirsuta capillis.
His certamen erat cuculi de carmine grande.

Ver prior adlusit ternos modulamine versus:
"Opto meus veniat cuculus, carissimus ales!   10
Omnibus iste solet fieri gratissimus hospes
in tectis modulans rutilo bona carmina rostro."

Tum glacialis Hiems respondit voce severa:
"Non veniat cuculus, nigris sed dormiat antris;
iste famem secum semper portare suescit."   15

Ver: "Opto meus veniat cuculus cum germine laeto,
frigora depellat, Foebo comis almus in aevum.
Foebus amat cuculum crescenti luce serena."

Hiems: "Non veniat cuculus, generat quia forte labores,
proelia congeminat, requiem disiungit amatam,   20
omnia disturbat: pelagi terraeque laborant."

Ver: "Quid tu, tarda Hiems, cuculo convitia cantas,
qui torpore gravi tenebrosis tectus in antris
post epulas Veneris, post stulti pocula Bacchi?"

Hiems: "Sunt mihi divitiae, sunt et convivia laeta,   25
est requies dulcis, calidus est ignis in aede.
Haec cuculus nescit, sed perfidus ille laborat."

Ver: "Ore feret flores cuculus et mella ministrat,
aedificatque domus, placidas et navigat undas,
et generat soboles, laetos et vestiet agros."   30

Hiems: "Haec inimica mihi sunt, quae tibi laeta videntur,
sed placet optatas gazas numerare per arcas
et gaudere cibis simul et requiescere semper."

Ver: "Quis tibi, tarda Hiems, semper dormire parata,
divitias cumulat, gazas vel congregat ullas,   35

si ver vel aestas ante tibi nulla laborant?"

Hiems: "Vera refers: illi, quoniam mihi multa laborant,
sunt etiam servi nostra ditione subacti,
iam mihi servantes domino quaecumque laborant."

Ver: "Non illis dominus, sed pauper inopsque superbus,   40
nec te iam poteris per te tu pascere tantum,
ni tibi qui veniet cuculus alimonia praestet."

Tum respondit ovans sublimi e sede Palemon
et Dafnis pariter, pastorum et turba piorum:
"Desine plura, Hiems; rerum tu prodigus atrox,   45
et veniet cuculus, pastorum dulcis amicus.
Collibus in nostris erumpant germina laeta,
pascua sit pecori, requies et dulcis in arvis;
et virides rami praestant umbracula fessis,
uberibus plenis veniuntque ad mulctra capellae,   50
et volucres varia Phoebum sub voce salutant.
Quapropter citius cuculus nunc ecce venito!
Tu iam dulcis amor, cunctis gratissimus hospes,
omnia te expectant, pelagus tellusque polusque.
Salve, dulce decus, cuculus, per saecula salve!"   55

Commentary

This poem is the earliest and best known Carolingian example of two
forms of poetry inherited from the classical past and highly influential in the
later Middle Ages: pastoral poetry and the debate poem; these forms may,
but need not, be combined into one as they are here. The author was
probably the Englishman Alcuin (d. 804), who left York in 781/2 to join
the circle of poets and scholars that Charlemagne was gathering at his court
in France. By his extensive writing in prose and verse, by his teaching (at
York, then at Aachen, and finally at St. Martin of Tours), and by his role as
advisor to Charlemagne, Alcuin was an influential figure in the Carolingian
"Renaissance," the revival in literature and learning encouraged by the
Frankish king. A few of Alcuin's poems (e.g., *Quae te dextra mihi rapuit
luscinia OBMLV* #78; *O mea cella OBMLV* #80) are noteworthy for a
remarkable fusion of classical and Christian language and ideas, for moving
personal expression, and for use of symbolic language. *Conveniunt subito
cuncti* is apparently less personal and more purely secular. There are
varying interpretations. Green calls the poem the "harbinger of a
millennium of North European May Day poetry," and points out that the
arrival of the cuckoo is an important event in folk-lore; certainly the almost
purely secular tone, unusual for Alcuin, foreshadows the imagery of
springtime very popular in later medieval poetry. Godman stresses

ambiguities in the debate and the flaws of *both* seasons' arguments; he maintains that the wit and the cut and thrust of debate are more important than the subject under discussion. Walsh suggests, in his general discussion of medieval pastoral, that the Christian sense of *pastor* is so intertwined with the classical genre in medieval pastoral that it would require a conscious effort to exclude Christian allusion. Certainly, at the level of connotation, the cuckoo as figure of life and rebirth might be suggestive of Christ; while the moral dimension of the dialogue (notably Winter's love of physical pleasures and his avarice) and some of the vocabulary (*perfidus, alimonia, salve per saecula*) might enhance this allusion (cf. Walsh's discussion of *Plangamus cuculum*, also probably by Alcuin). There has been some doubt of Alcuin's authorship of this poem, but Green and others adduce strong arguments for its authenticity.

Ms.: The popularity of *Conveniunt subito cuncti* is reflected by the number of extant mss. in which it is found; Dümmler cites 15, six of them from the ninth century. There are numerous small variations, particularly in spelling and the use of the subjunctive, that make the determination of an exact text difficult.

Meter: Quantitative; hexameters. The syllabic scansion is generally accurate, though there occur examples of the ML treatment of h (allowing hiatus in 22, 34, 45) and the lengthening of a final short syllable under the ictus (26, 28, 42; for 36, cf. below, *ad. loc.*). According to Green (p. 37), the occurrence of these exceptions is only slightly more frequent than in Alcuin's other works. The structure of the verse is classical. Elision occurs four times (43, 44, 50, 54). There is no rhyme.

Bibliography: R.P.H. Green, *Seven Versions of Carolingian Pastoral*, University of Reading, 1980; Godman, pp. 16-22, pp. 144-149; also, Godman, "Alcuin's Poetic Style and the Authenticity of 'O mea Cella,'" *Studi Medievali*, Ser. 3, v. 20, pt. 2 (1979) 555-583; *OBMLV* # 75; E. Dümmler, *Poetae Latini Aevi Carolini*, v.1 (1881), pp. 270-2; J.I. McEnerney, "Alcuin, Carmen 58," *Mittellateinisches Jahrbuch*, 16 (1981) 35-42; P.G. Walsh, "*Pastor* and Pastoral in Medieval Latin Poetry," in F. Cairns, ed., *Papers of the Liverpool Latin Seminar 1976*, Liverpool, 1977, pp. 157-169; Wilhelm, pp. 88-94.

1	**conveniunt:** For a similar gathering of shepherds, cf. Virg. *Ecl.* 10.16-27. Green notes that the landscape details are imitated from earlier poetry (e.g., *de montibus altis,* common in Virgil), except for *vernali luce* which is apparently original. On the whole of this poem, the influence of Virgil's eclogues is particularly strong; the later Roman pastoral poets, Calpurnius and Nemesianus, are also echoed.
2	**vernali luce:** "in the spring sunshine" (Green); ablative of time.
3	**pariter:** "together."
	celebrare: See *Linguistic Note* (Infinitive 1). Here, with *Camenas,* "to celebrate the Muses, sing songs."

Camenas: originally Roman goddesses, perhaps water deities, especially connected with a grove outside the Porta Capena in Rome; later identified with the Muses (*OLD*).

4 **Dafnis ... Palemon:** in CL orthography, *Daphnis* and *Palaemon*. Both are characters in Virgil's eclogues (e.g., 2, 5, 7; Palaemon is the judge figure in 3) and in later pastoral.

senior: Both classical and medieval influences are at work. There is often a difference of age in singers in Virgilian and later pastoral (Virg. *Ecl.* 1, 4, 6; Nemesianus 1; cf. Green *ad. loc.*). "Senior" to a medieval audience was a term of respect, e.g., "lord" (*MLLM*; cf., e.g., Spanish *señor*). A later Carolingian pastoral poet, Modoin, with perhaps a reference to this well-known poem, identified Charlemagne with Palemon (Green, p. 37, No. 4.24).

5 **cuculo:** "cuckoo." The first arrival of the cuckoo is still eagerly watched for in Britain (it first appeared on Feb. 26th in 1952; *The New Caxton Encyclopedia*, "Cuckoo," vol. 6, p. 1726, London, 1969); the cuckoo thus is a fitting symbol for spring throughout the following lines.

6-7 Cf. the descriptions of Spring and Winter in the court of Phoebus in Ovid *Met.* 2.27 and 30: *Verque novum stabat cinctum florente corona; et glacialis Hiems canos hirsuta capillos.* Scholars debate as to whether or not Alcuin was familiar with Ovid; in any case, the writer of this poem, if he is in fact influenced by this Ovidian passage, could have had access to it through anthologies or through quotation by an intermediate author.

6 **Ver:** masculine (*succinctus*, cf. 9) while in CL it is neuter. For *Hiems*, there is confusion in gender: feminine in 7, 22, 34, but masculine in 23, 39, 40, 45; apparently the *persona* of *Hiems* was intended to be masculine, but the grammatical gender of *hiems* occasionally took priority. McEnerney sees the *persona* of *Hiems* as feminine and reinterprets the poem in this light; to do so, he emends all uses of the masculine for *Hiems* throughout the poem: e.g., *quae torpore gravi tenebrosis tecta es in antris*, 23; *dominae*, 39; *non illis domina es, sed pauper inopsque superba*, 40; *prodiga et atrox*, 45

florigero ... stemmate: *florigero* is not CL; cf. *Linguistic Note* (Adjectives 1). *Stemma*, in CL "family tree, lineage," here = "crown" (*MLLM*).

succinctus: perfect passive participle of *succingo*, "bound."

8 **his:** refers to *Ver* and *Hiems*.

certamen: Cf. Virg. *Ecl.* 7.16: *et certamen erat Corydon cum Thyrside magnum*; Calpurnius (2.9) also imitates Virgil, replacing *magnum* with LL *grande* ("big").

9 **adlusit:** "playfully sang" (Godman); < *alludo*, "play or sport with."

ternos: "three" (possibly, "three at a time" or "three each").

modulamine: "with modulation or melody," i.e., "melodiously."

10	**veniat:** with an understood *ut*, after *opto*.
11	**iste:** Cf. *Linguistic Note* (Pronouns 1),

omnibus: "to all men"; with this line compare 53.

fieri: = *esse*.

12   **modulans ... carmina:** Cf. Virg. *Ecl.* 5. 14 (*carmina descripsi et modulans alterna notavi*) and 10.51 (*carmina pastoris Siculi modulabor avena*); *modulans* < *modulor*, "set to music."

rutilo ... rostro: "red beak."

13   **glacialis Hiems:** Cf. above on 6-7, also Virg. *Aen.* 3.285.

14-5   There may be a line missing in *Hiems'* song, since the other song exchanges are all of 3 lines (cf. 9), but there is no ms. support for this and there is no need to assume absolute symmetry.

14   **non:** *ne* would be usual with the hortatory subjunctive in CL.

nigris ... antris: ablative of place where, freely used in poetry without the preposition *in*.

15   **iste ... suescit:** The cuckoo "brings famine" because in spring the food stored from the previous harvest might be exhausted; the hard work (cf. 19) of spring planting would be necessary to replenish the food supply.

secum ... suescit: Cf. Alcuin *Carmen* 26.51 (= Godman #7): *qui secum tunnam semper portare suescit* (a description of the cupbearer at Charlemagne's court, who always carries a barrel, *tunna*, with him).

16   **germine:** < *germen*, "sprout, bud."

17   **Foebo:** = CL *Phoebus* (cf. *Linguistic Note*, Orthography 6); dative of reference.

comis: CL *comes;* cf. *Linguistic Note* (Orthography 1).

in aevum: "forever, for all eternity."

18   **crescenti ... serena:** ablative absolute. "The sense is that the sun beams approvingly on the cuckoo as the days become longer" (Green).

19   **quia:** postponed conjunction, as often in poetry; should logically precede *generat*.

forte: probably a metrical filler, or (Green's suggestion) "for instance."

20   Campaigning began in the spring.

22   **quid:** = "why?"

tarda Hiems: See above, **Meter**. *Tarda* = "lingering, dull-witted," or "obstructive."

convitia: CL *convicium*, "angry noise, abuse"; cf. *Linguistic Note* (Orthography 3).

23   **tectus:** with an ellipse of *es; tectus es* (< *tego*, "cover, hide,") is the verb of the clause *qui ... Bacchi*. Various emendations have been proposed: *stertis* (Schenkl, based on *tectis* in one ms.; "you snore") is the most attractive; also see above on 6.

24   **stulti:** perhaps, "stultifying."

pocula Bacchi: Cf. Virg. *Aen.* 3.354.

25ff.   These lines seem to be modeled on Virg. *Georgics*1.300 ff (a description of the delights that *genialis hiems* offers the farmer).
         mihi: dative of possession.

26   **calidus:** For the lengthening of a short syllable under the ictus, see **Meter.**

27   **perfidus:** in CL "treacherous, deceitful"; here, "disbelieving, heretical" (*MLLM*). See *Linguistic Note* (Vocabulary 1).

28-30   This is an answer to 19-21 above, and a list of items that blends the activities of the cuckoo with what the arrival of spring causes men or nature to do.
         feret ... vestiet: futures used for the present, probably for metrical convenience.

29   **domus:** accusative plural.

30   **soboles:** CL *suboles*, "children"; rare in CL in the plural.

32   **placet:** Understand *mihi* from 31.
         gazas: "treasure."
         per arcas: *in arcis* ("chests") would be the CL phrase.

33   **cibis:** ablative with *gaudere*.

36   **vel ... ante:** In both words the e is lengthened under the ictus, though neither word falls at the main caesura. *Vel* may be an erroneous substitute for *aut*, because of the preceding *ver* (Green, *ad. loc.*).

37   **vera refers:** Cf. Ovid *Met.* 5.271. Note the pun *vera/ver*.

38   **etiam:** "actually" (with a word or phrase expressing a more extreme case, *OLD*).
         ditione: < CL *dicio*, "authority, power."
         subacti: < *subigo*, "subdue."

39   **domino:** in apposition to *mihi*.
         quaecumque laborant: "all they labor to produce" (Godman).

40-42   The first speaker, Spring, also speaks last, which is not customary in the amoebaeans (alternating songs) of classical pastoral. *OBMLV* incorrectly omits 37-39, and therefore, also incorrectly, gives 40-42 to Winter.

40   **illis:** dative of reference.
         superbus: probably, an example of the frequent use of adjectives for nouns in ML; possibly the placing of *-que* is misunderstood and there is a list of 3 adjectives here. *Es* is to be understood as the verb.

41   **nec ... tantum:** "and ... not even."

42   **ni:** = *nisi*, "unless.
         alimonia: < *alimonium*, "food"; Green suggests irony here, as this is the term for charitable support for the weak.
         praestet: In future conditions, a present subjunctive may sometimes stand in the protasis with the future indicative (*poteris* 41) in the apodosis; this might be considered a mixed more vivid / less vivid condition.

43   **respondit:** There are in effect 3 subjects: *Palemon, Dafnis, and pastorum ... turba*; as often, the verb is singular to agree with the nearest subject.

        ovans: "rejoicing."

45-55   The final description represents an ideal landscape (*locus amoenus*), a conventional theme used for varying effects in CL and ML poetry (Curtius, pp. 183 ff.; Wilhelm, pp. 39-42 and *passim*). Earlier themes are recalled and redefined, by words and phrases such as *rerum ... prodigus, requies* (cf. *umbracula*), *Phoebum, gratissimus hospes*, etc.

45   **desine plura:** Cf. Virg. *Ecl.* 5.19 (*Sed tu desine plura, puer; successimus antro*), 9.66 (*Desine plura, puer, et quod nunc instat agamus*).

        rerum ... atrox: Understand *es. Rerum ... prodigus:* "squanderer of wealth" (Godman).

46-49   Green defends (despite many editors' doubts) the sequence of tenses of *veniet* 46 ... *erumpant* 47 ... *sit* 48; *veniet* appears in most mss., *erumpant* and *sit* in almost all.

48   **pascua:** feminine singular (as often in ML), rather than CL neuter plural.

49-51   Most mss. support the present tenses *praestant ... veniunt ... salutant*, though most editors read hortatory subjunctives. Green, accepting the presents, suggests that these lines mark the turning point of the poem "as Nature underlines their (Palemon's and the shepherds') judgement and Spring visibly arrives."

49   **umbracula:** < *umbraculum;* poetic plural. Cf. Virg. *Ecl.* 9.42 (with its parenthetical phrase ... *et lentae texunt umbracula vites*); shade is a *topos* of the ideal pastoral landscape.

50   **veniuntque ad mulctra capellae:** Cf. Hor. *Epode* 16.49 (*veniunt ad mulctra capellae*). There is little evidence that a text of Horace was available in England or France at this period; cf. above on 6-7.

        uberibus: < *uber*, "teat."

        mulctra: < *mulctrum*, "milking-pail."

51   **sub voce:** In CL this would be expressed with an ablative of means; cf. *Linguistic Note* (Prepositions 2).

52   **quapropter:** "therefore."

        citius: "quickly." See *Linguistic Note* (Adjectives 2).

        venito: future imperative.

53   **dulcis amor:** Cf. Sedulius Scottus *Hymni* 1.82.

54   **polus:** "sky."

55   **dulce decus:** "sweet beauty"; this phrase is used by Horace (*Carm.* 1.1.1) and is imitated by Venantius Fortunatus (*Carm.* 11.5.1 and *passim*).

No. 6
Angilbert: Aurora cum primo mane

Aurora cum primo mane tetra noctis dividit,   s.1
sabbati non illud fuit sed Saturni dolium.
De fraterna rupta pace gaudet demon impius.

Bella clamant. Hinc et inde pugna gravis oritur.   s.2
Frater fratri mortem parat, nepoti avunculus,
filius nec patri suo exhibet quod meruit.

Cedes nulla peior fuit campo nec in Marcio.   s.3
Fracta est lex christianorum; sanguinis hic profluit
unda manans; inferorum gaudet gula Cerberi.

Dextera prepotens dei protexit Hlotharium,   s.4
victor ille manu sua pugnavitque fortiter.
Ceteri si sic pugnassent, mox foret victoria.

Ecce olim velut Iudas salvatorem tradidit,   s.5
sic te, rex, tuique duces tradiderunt gladio.
Esto cautus, ne frauderis agnus lupo previus.

Fontaneto fontem dicunt, villam quoque rustice,   s.6
ubi strages et ruina Francorum de sanguine.
Orrent campi, orrent silve, orrent ipsi paludes.

Gramen illud ros et ymber nec humectet pluvia,   s.7
in quo fortes ceciderunt, prelio doctissimi,
pater, mater, soror, frater, quos amici fleverant.

Hoc autem scelus peractum, quod descripsi ritmice,   s.8
Angelbertus ego vidi pugnansque cum aliis,
solus de multis remansi prima frontis acie.

Ima vallis retrospexi in collis cacumine,   s.9
ubi suos inimicos rex fortis Hlotharius
debellabat fugientes usque foras rivulum.

Karoli de parte vero, Hludovici pariter,   s.10
albescunt campi vestimentis mortuorum lineis,
velut solent in autumno albescere avibus.

Laude pugna non est digna, nec canatur melode.   s.11
Oriens, meridianus, occidens et aquilo
plangant illos qui fuerunt tali pena mortui.

Maledictus ille dies, nec in anni circulo   s.12
numeretur, sed radatur ab omni memoria,
iubar solis nec illustrat aurore crepusculum.

Nox et sequens dies illam, nox que dira nimium,   s.13
nox illa, que planctu mixta et dolore pariter,
hic obit et ille gemit cum in gravi peniuria.

O luctum atque lamentum! Nudati sunt mortui;   s.14
illorum carnes vultur, corvus, lupus vorant acriter.
Orrent, carent sepulturis, vanum iacet cadaver.

Ploratum et ululatum nec describo amplius.   s.15
Unusquisque quantum potest restringatque lacrimas.
Pro illorum animabus deprecemur Dominum.

Commentary

Aurora cum primo mane, a lament (*planctus*) in a tradition derived from the Bible but adapted in the Carolingian period for secular subjects, was written by an otherwise unknown Angilbert (to be distinguished from the well-known Angilbert, poet, courtier, and friend of Alcuin). As he tells us himself, he was a participant at the battle of Fontenoy (near Auxerre, France) on June 25, 841, where Lothar (whose follower Angilbert was), eldest son of Louis the Pious, was defeated by his younger brothers Charles the Bald and Louis the German. This conflict is typical of the divisive struggles among the descendants of Charlemagne.   Poems about contemporary political events were a new and characteristic development of Carolingian literature. Godman (pp. 48-50), criticizing scholars who try to define this poem as either "popular" (and influenced by the vernacular German ballad) or "learned," sees this work as typical of Carolingian Latin rhythmical poetry in which the authors are intentionally trying to write in the Latin spoken by clerics of their own day, a distinctive *lingua franca* neither "popular" nor wholly "learned."

Ms.: This song is preserved in three mss., one of the tenth century (Paris ms. lat. 1154) and two of the ninth century (the Fabariensis and the Kornikanus 124). The first is the famous ms. from the abbey of Saint-Martial in Limoges, the earliest extant ms. to preserve Latin verse with its music; this ms. gives an idea of the wide musical repertoire of the period: hymns, songs with Biblical themes and current battle themes (as in *Aurora cum primo mane*, battle song as well as lament, complete with musical notation), dirges (*planctus*, e.g. one for Charlemagne), three poems from Boethius' *Consolation of Philosophy* set to music, and four religious lyrics by Gottschalk (see No. 7). The wide variations between texts in the three manuscripts may be due to differences of oral transmission. Examples of versions different from those of Norberg and Godman, who usually follow Kornikanus 124, are:

s.3.2-3: ... ...*sanguinis proluvio,*
　　　　unde manus inferorum, gaudet gula Cerberi.
s.9.3　*expugnabat fugientes usque forum rivuli.*
s.13　*Noxque illa, nox amara, noxque dura nimium,*
　　　　in qua fortes ceciderunt, proelio doctissimi,
　　　　pater, mater, soror, frater, quos amici fleverant.

(According to this version, the last two lines cited appear twice in the poem.)

Meter: Rhythmical. The pattern of the stanza: 3 x (8p + 7pp). This is a rhythmic imitation of the trochaic septenarius (its quantitative pattern: -u-u-u-u // -u-u-u-) well-known from Venantius Fortunatus' hymn *Pange lingua.* This rhythmic pattern, and the alphabetic beginning of each stanza as an aid to the memory for oral performance, are typical of religious music of the eighth and ninth centuries. [There are occasional extra syllables in either half of the line (cf. s.10.2, s.13.3, s.14.2; *Christianorum* s.3.2 is an example of synizesis); there are also exceptions to the paroxytone and proparoxytone patterns (cf. s.6.3, s.14.3, possibly s.11.1).] There is no rhyme and no elision.

Bibliography: Godman, pp. 48-50, 262-265; Norberg, *Manuel,* pp. 166-9; *OBMLV* #83; *Poetae Latini Aevi Carolini,* v. 2, 137-9.

s.1.1　**aurora:** Angilbert seems to be consciously imitating classical epic, which initiates important scenes with reference to the arrival of dawn.
　　　cum: the conjunction, postponed.
　　　primo mane: "in the very early morning."
　　　tetra: < CL *taeter -tra -trum,* "foul, horrible" (often used of smell, taste, sound). Here, the plural of the neuter adjective is used as a noun (see *Linguistic Note,* Nouns 4).
　　　dividit: either a present used in place of a perfect, perhaps on the analogy of the usage of tenses with *dum,* or a mistaken form of the perfect (instead of the CL *divisit),* in which case the word accent may be irregular, i.e., not proparoxytone.

2　　　**Sabbati:** sc. *dies,* "Saturday"; the battle occurred on a Saturday. (At this period, the term "Sabbath" had not yet been transferred to Sunday). There is sound play with *Sabbati ... Saturni,* and also a contrast between the Christian and pagan names for the day of the week.
　　　Saturni dolium: Instead of the expected "*dies,*" *dolium* (a large container, "cauldron") is substituted. Norberg (*Manuel,* p. 171) suggests the image of hell's cauldron and quotes an early medieval writer (in M.C. Diáz of Diáz, *Anecdota Wisigothica,* I, Salamanca, 1958, p. 113): *vereantur voraginis urnam sine fine urentem.*

3　　　**de ... pace:** In this construction, the perfect passive participle (*rupta* < *rumpo*) is best translated as a noun, "the breaking of ... "

De indicates cause, with *gaudet,* as occasionally in CL and often in ML.

fraterna: See introductory note.

demon: "devil."

s.2.1   **bella clamant:** The plural of *bellum* (here, "fighting, battle," or, with a spatial sense, "the area of battle") probably indicates the different parts of the battle line or the two sides in the fratricidal struggle.

2   **nepoti:** in ML "nephew" (as here) or "first cousin" (in CL, "grandson").

avunculus: = "uncle."

3   **quod meruit:** lit., "what (the father) has earned," i.e., "deserves."

s.3.1   **cedes:** CL *caedes;* see *Linguistic Note* (Orthography 1).

nulla ... nec: One of these negatives is superfluous; Norberg suggests the influence of the spoken language, in which double negatives added emphasis rather than cancelling each other out. *Nec:* In ML, *et* is often superfluous; *nec* = *non.* Angilbert inserts *et* and *-que* superfluously (e.g., s.5.2).

peior: comparative of *malus.*

campo ... Marcio: Not the Roman Campus Martius, but, generally, any battlefield.

3   **manans:** < *mano,* "flow, drip, spread."

inferorum: < *inferi, -orum,* in CL "the dead, the underworld," in ML "hell." Genitive with *Cerberi,* "dog of hell."

Cerberi: the three-headed dog of classical myth, to whom the dead had to offer a cake before entering the underworld.

s.4.1   **prepotens:** CL *praepotens,* "very powerful."

Hlotharium: Lothar.

2   **victor ... manu sua:** Lothar was personally brave, though his army was defeated.

-que: either sc. *erat* with *victor ... sua,* or *-que* is postponed; in prose, it would stand after *victor.*

3   **foret:** variant form for imperfect subjunctive *esset.* In CL the pluperfect subjunctive would be expected here; see *Linguistic Note* (Subjunctive 3).

s.5.1   **Iudas:** the Biblical Judas.

2   **-que:** superfluous; do not translate.

3   **esto:** imperative of *esse.*

previus: CL *praevius,* "going before," i.e., "meeting" (the wolf).

s.6.1   **Fontaneto:** Fontenoy, accusative in apposition to *fontem.*

villam quoque: "also the town nearby."

rustice: "in the vernacular."

2   **strages:** "destruction, slaughter." Understand *erant* with *strages* and *ruina*.

      de: with *sanguine*; see *Linguistic Note* (Prepositions 1).

3   **orrent:** CL *horrent;* see *Linguistic Note* (Orthography 7).

      silve: CL *silvae.*

      ipsi: either emphatic, "the very (swamps)," or superfluous and to be omitted in translation.

s.7.1   Cf. the sorrow of David in 2 *Samuel* 1.21 (*Montes Gelboe, nec ros, nec pluvia veniant super vos ...*).

      gramen illud: object of *humectat.*

      et ... nec: In CL *nec* would appear before each of the three nouns: *nec ros ... nec imber ... nec pluvia* (cf. s.12.3); the omission of *nec* in such phrases is a typical ML variant .

      ymber: CL *imber*, "shower (of rain)." See *Linguistic Note* (Orthography 1).

      humectet: < *umectare*, "to moisten."

      pluvia: "rain."

2   **prelio:** CL *proelio (praelio)*, "battle"; ablative with *doctissimi;* cf. 1 *Maccabees* 4.7 and 6.30 (*docti ad praelium*).

3   **pater ... frater:** all subjects, with *amici*, of the clause *quos ... fleverant.*

s.8.1   **peractum:** perfect passive participle < *perago*, modifying *scelus*; translate as a noun "the completion of (this crime)" (cf. on s.1.3).

      ritmice: "in rhythmical verse" (Godman); in CL, *rhythmicus* or *rythmicus*, from Greek = ῥυθμικός.

2   **Angelbertus ego vidi:** It was unusual, though by no means unknown, for a medieval poet to name himself.

      prima frontis acie: pleonastic; either *prima frons* or *prima acies* = "front line."

s.9.1   **ima:** adjective used as a noun; see above on s.1.1.

      retrospexi: < *retrospicio*, "look back at"; see *Linguistic Note* (Vocabulary 4).

      in: In CL *de* would be the expected preposition.

3   **debellabat:** "was subduing."

      usque foras: "up to and beyond," i.e., "to the other side of." *Foras* is here a preposition with the accusative (= CL *ultra*) ; see *Linguistic Note* (Prepositions).

      rivulum: "small stream."

s.10.1   **Karoli:** Charles (the Bald).

      de parte: "on the side of."

      Hludovici pariter: Understand *de parte*: "and in the same way on the side of Louis (the German)."

2   **albescunt:** "become white."

mortuorum: adjective (actually, perfect participle of *morior*) used as noun, "the dead."

s.11.1   **laude**: ablative with *digna*.

canatur: possibly hortatory subjunctive, or perhaps with an idea of obligation or propriety, which in CL would be conveyed by the gerundive or *oportet*.

melode: an adverb from LL *melodus -a -um*, "melodious"; in CL only as a neuter plural noun *meloda* (from Greek μελῳδός), "poetry, songs."

2   **Oriens ... aquilo**: i.e., the four points of the compass.

3   **fuerunt ... mortui**: CL *mortui sunt;* cf. *Linguistic Note* (Tenses 5).

pena: CL *poena;* in ML, "suffering, pain."

ss.12-13 Cf *Jeremiah* 20.14: *Maledicta dies in qua natus sum*; *Job* 3.4-7: *Dies ille ... non illustretur lumine ... non computetur in diebus anni ... Sit nox illa solitaria nec laude digna ...*

s.12.1   **maledictus**: sc. *sit*.

in anni circulo: a Biblical expression (cf. *Leviticus* 25.3).

2   **radatur**: "erase."

3   **iubar solis**: *nec* is to be understood with this phrase, which is parallel to *nec ... crepusculum* and also the subject of *illustrat* (see above on s.7.1).

illustrat: probably in error for hortatory subjunctive *illustret*.

aurore: CL *aurorae*, genitive with *crepusculum*, perhaps to be translated as "half-light" (cf. s.1.1); in LL *crepusculum* = "dawn," while in CL "twilight, dusk."

s.13.1   **nox ... dies**: sc. *Maledictus sit* from the previous stanza.

que: = CL *quae;* as in the next line.

dira: sc. *est*.

2   **mixta**: sc. *est*.

3   **cum**: postponed conjunction; translate before *hic*.

peniuria: in CL *penuria*, "dearth, want"; here probably, "suffering," cf. on *pena* s.11.3 above.

s.14.1   **lamentum**: "wailing, weeping"; neuter singular, in CL only in neuter plural.

nudati sunt: < *nudare*, "to strip naked."

mortui: See above on s.10.2.

2   **carnes**: < *caro*, "flesh"; in LL, "human body." Both meanings are appropriate here.

acriter: "fiercely, savagely."

3   **orrent**: See above on s.6.3. The meaning: "be (become) stiff."

sepulturis: ablative with *carent* ("be without").

vanum: "ineffectual," i.e., "helpless."

s.15.1 Cf. *Matthew* 2.18: *Ploratus et ululatus multus: / Rachel plorans filios suos* and *Jeremiah* 3.21: *Ploratus et ululatus filiorum Israel.*

  nec: for *non;* see above on s.3.1.

  describo: present for the future, as often in ML.

2 **unusquisque:** "each one."

  quantum potest: "as much as he can."

  -que: superfluous.

3 **animabus:** an old form of the first declension dative and ablative plural, rare except *deabus* and *filiabus.*

  deprecemur: < *deprecor,* "pray, beg mercy for."

No. 7
Gottschalk: Ut quid iubes

Ut quid iubes, pusiole,   s.1
quare mandas, filiole,
      carmen dulce me cantare,
      cum sim longe exul valde
         intra mare?   5
        O cur iubes canere?

Magis mihi, miserule,   s.2
flere libet, puerule,
      plus plorare quam cantare
      carmen tale, iubes quale,
         amor care.   5
        O cur iubes canere?

Mallem scias, pusillule,   s.3
ut velles tu, fratercule,
      pio corde condolere
      mihi atque prona mente
         conlugere.   5
        O cur iubes canere?

Scis, divine tyruncule,   s.4
scis, superne clientule,
      hic diu me exulare,
      multa die sive nocte
         tolerare.   5
        O cur iubes canere?

Scis captive plebicule   s.5
Israheli cognomine
      praeceptum in Babilone
      decantare extra longe
         fines Iude.   5
        O cur iubes canere?

Non potuerunt utique   s.6
nec debuerunt itaque
      carmen dulce coram gente
      aliene nostri terre
         resonare.   5
        O cur iubes canere?

Sed quia vis omnimode,   s.7
o sodalis egregie,

canam patri filioque
simul atque procedente
 ex utroque.   5
  Hoc cano ultronee.

"Benedictus es, Domine,   s.8
pater, nate, paraclite,
 deus trine, deus une,
 deus summe, deus pie,
  deus iuste."   5
  Hoc cano spontanee.

"Exul ego diuscule   s.9
hoc in mari sum, Domine,
 annos nempe duos fere
 nosti fore, sed iam iamque
  miserere."   5
  Hoc rogo humillime.

"Plenus enim facinore   s.10
ego sum, o rex optime,
 pleniorem sectae verae
 pietatem novi esse
  fateorque."   5
  Hoc credo firmissime.

"Propterea, piissime,   s.11
miserere iam, Domine,
 pietatis rector clare,
 famulique, rex aeterne,
  memorare."   5
  Prono posco pectore.

"Reduc me velocissime,   s.12
o ductor clementissime.
 Nolo hic me magis esse,
 pater sancte, flatus alme
  veridice."   5
  Hoc rogo praecipue.

Interim cum pusione   s.13
situs hac in regione,
 psallam ore, psallam corde,
 psallam die, psallam nocte
  carmen dulce   5
  tibi, rex piissime.

Commentary

This religious lyric was written by Gottschalk (d. 869), a poet remarkable in his period for his complexity of rhythm and rhyme and original in his creation of a sense of "personal presence" and emotional expressiveness. Entered very young as a novice at Fulda, Gottschalk attempted to escape from his monastic vows (829), travelled extensively in Europe as preacher and theologian, was condemned for an heretical doctrine on predestination (849), and was confined to the monastery of Hautvilliers until his death. *Ut quid iubes* is structured as an address to a young friend who has asked the poet for a "sweet song." Scholars have attempted to link the poem to situations in the poet's life (e.g., an unhappy stay at the monastery of Reichenau, *ca.* 825) and to identify the friend. But, the amount of autobiographical fact included in the poem is irrelevant; Gottschalk appears to be utilizing the form of address to a friend, a favorite medieval *topos*, as a strategy for the expression of his ideas. Possibly, the *persona* of the friend for whom he is writing is to be interpreted as an *alter ego* (Godman, p. 42) and the poem as one of inner debate. The first 6 stanzas convey Gottschalk's lament for his exile and his inability to sing the song asked for, the seventh, central, stanza offers a different type of song, and the last 6 stanzas present the revised song, one of contrition for sin, plea for divine mercy, and praise for the Trinity (cf. similar themes in Gottschalk's other poems, *OBMLV* #90, #91, and *O mi custos*, Godman #34).

Ms.: The text of *Ut quid iubes* depends on 5 mss. Four are incomplete: Paris B.N. 1154 (see above on No. 6, Ms.), which includes the melody for the song, Autun 33, both ninth century, Montpellier Fac. Med. 219, tenth century, and Paris B.N. Lat. 12140, fol. 2v, tenth century and also with the melody. In the fifth ms. (Angers 477, second half of the ninth century, offically containing works of Bede and other texts), originally only the first half of the poem was noticed; in 1965, the rest of the poem, including 3 stanzas never before known and a correct text of the last stanza, was discovered, inserted in a convenient empty spot 5 pages further along in the text. This discovery removed misconceptions about the poem and has allowed a better understanding of it. (*OBMLV* # 92 and *Poetae Latini Aevi Carolini* v.3, pp. 731-2, contain the mutilated, pre-1965 text).

Meter: Rhythmic. The pattern: 2 x (4p + 4pp) + 2 x (4p + 4p) + 4p + **Refr.:** 7pp. There are a number of exceptions to the pattern of word stress: the fixed caesura in lines 1 and 2 (s.12.1-2); the paroxytone caesura accent of lines 1-2 (e.g., s.3.2, s.7.1) and proparoxytone end accent of lines 1-2 (s.6.1, s.13.1-2); the accents of lines 3-4 and line 5 (s.4.3, s.5.3, s.12.5). Klopsch (p. 87) suggests that at this early period much of the rhythmic effect depended on the melody. All lines end with assonance in e, many words before the caesura also end in e, and there are many instances of two-syllable rhyme, which is unusual for the ninth century. No elision.

Bibliography: B. Bischoff, "Gottschalks Lied fur den Reichenauer Freund," *Mittelalterliche Studien*, 3 vols., Stuttgart, 1966-1981, vol. 2, pp. 26-34; P. Diehl, *The Medieval European Religious Lyric*, Berkeley, University of California Press, 1985; Dronke, *ML*, London, 1968, pp. 34-6, p. 231 (the melody); Godman, pp. 39-43, 228-32; P. Klopsch, "Die Mittellateinische Lyrik," *Lyrik des Mittelalters*, ed. by H. Bergner, Stuttgart, 1983, v.1, pp. 71-94; Raby, *SLP*, v. 1, pp. 226-8.

s.1.1 **Ut quid:** "why?"

  pusiole: vocative < *pusiolus* (diminutive of *pusio*, "boy"). A series of diminutives (also vocatives) falls at the end of the first 2 lines of the first 4 stanzas. The emotional tone of the terms used of the young (masculine) friend is open to interpretation. Dronke has pointed out (*ML*, pp. 192 ff.) that the "*courtoisie* of friendship" regularly elicited passionate, even erotic language for non-erotic relationships; following the lead of church fathers such as Ambrose, a cleric, without amatory intent, could write a nun phrases such as "*Crede mihi, quia te summo conplector amore,*" and "*Vale Christo virguncula, Christi nempe tiruncula, mihi care magnopere* ... " However, J. Boswell (*Christianity, Social Tolerance, and Homosexuality*, Chicago, 1980) suggests that "gay sensibilities" are reflected in some of these clerical expressions of affection; he says of *Ut quid iubes* "It is virtually impossible to translate the affection suggested by the series of diminutives at the end of the lines of this poem ... They are part of a tradition of erotic address between men which has no standard terms of relation and has thus elicited the ambiguities of the ... monastic 'brother, son, friend, beloved brother' and many other terms of endearment for relationships without real parallel in heterosexual contexts" (p.193).

2 **quare:** "why?"; introducing a second main clause parallel to that in 1.

  filiole: < *filius;* see on *pusiole*, 1.

3 **carmen dulce:** This probably implies a pleasant, joyous song. Bischoff (p. 92) quotes Horace *Ars poetica* 99f. (*non satis est pulchra esse poemata: dulcia sunto / et quocumque volent animum auditoris agunto*), and suggests that part of the structure of this poem centers around the redefinition of a "sweet song."

4-5 **cum ... mare:** There is much scholarly speculation concerning the exile (his stay in Reichenau? Italy?) to which this refers in Gottschalk's wandering and troubled life. If Gottschalk wrote this poem ca. 825 in Reichenau, the situation of that monastery on an island in the Bodensee may well have suggested the sea imagery to him, and even the use of *intra mare* ("within the sea," i.e., "confined by the waters of the Bodensee") in 5. [Less persuasive is Raby's interpretation, *OBMLV* #92; he suggests (following the usage of Pomponius Mela the geographer) that the Mediterranean

	sea is implied, and translates *intra mare* as "within the region of the Mediterranean sea"].
4	**exul**: Both *exul* and *exsul* are correct spellings.
	valde: "assuredly" (emphasizes a whole sentence).
6	The refrain: Gottschalk frequently aims for an emotive use of repetition (e.g., *OBMLV* #91, *O deus miseri miserere servi*, repeated 20 times as introduction to 20 stanzas).

s.2.1-2	**mihi ... libet**: "it pleases me, I want."
3	**plorare**: a further infinitive dependent on *libet*, in asyndeton (i.e., without a connective such as *et*).
	quam: "than," comparative adverb after *magis* and *plus*.
4	**quale**: relative pronoun introducing *iubes*, "such as."
5	**amor care**: vocative.

s.3.1-2	**mallem ... velles**: Probably an *ut* is to be understood with *scias*; two clauses, in asyndeton, (*ut scias* and *ut velles*), are dependent on *mallem*: "I should like you to know ... to wish." "Knowing how to grieve", an apparently unusual concept, would refer to recognition and repentance for sin, which is the sorrow Gottschalk wishes his friend to share with him (cf. s. 10).
1	**mallem**: See *Linguistic Note* (Subjunctive 4).
	pusillule: < *pusillus*, "very small, very insignificant"; cf. on *pusiole*, 1.
2	**fratercule**: "little brother."
3-4	**condolere**: In CL appears only as *condolescere* ("grieve with"), in ML as *condolere*, "pity" (*MLLM*), + dative.
4	**prona**: "bending forward," i.e., "humble."
5	**conlugere**: "grieve with (me), sympathize with (me)." CL *lugere*, "grieve, lament." See *Linguistic Note* (Vocabulary 4).

s.4.1	**tyruncule**: "little novice." (In CL *tiro* was originally a newly recruited soldier, or a young man just come of age). (See *Linguistic Note*, Orthography 1).
2	**clientule**: In ML *cliens* often = "vassal, man-at-arms," but here the meaning is closer to CL, "client, dependent." Gottschalk uses *cliens* for himself in relation to God (*OBMLV* #90.19, #91.67 and 125) and describes himself with diminutives (*misellus*, #90.14, #91.117, *fraterculus*, Godman #34 s.43), in similar terms to those he uses for the addressee of this poem.
3	**multa**: accusative, object of *tolerare* ("suffer").
	die ... nocte: See *Linguistic Note* (Cases 2).

s.5.1	**captive plebicule**: not a vocative but dative (cf. *Linguistic Note*, Orthography 1) with *praeceptum (esse)*, < *praecipio*, "order." The allusion to the Babylonian Captivity of the Jews, and in particular to Psalm 136 (e.g., verse 4: *Quomodo cantabimus*

canticum Domini in terra aliena?) is an analogy for Gottschalk's state of spiritual suffering.

2	**Israheli cognomine:** "by name Israel."
4	**decantare:** = "sing" (*MLLM*).
5	**Iude:** CL *Iudae*, the land of Judah.
6	**O ... canere:** The refrain here and in s.6 takes on a new meaning.

s.6.1	**utique:** after a negative = "on any account, certainly (not)."
2	**resonare:** complementary infinitive to *potuerunt* and *debuerunt* .
3	**coram:** a preposition with ablative, "in the presence of, before."
4	**aliene ... terre:** genitive dependent on *gente*.

nostri: difficult to interpret; probably, genitive with *aliene terre*, as "a land foreign to us." With this interpretation, Gottschalk, who has identified the Jews' sorrow and inability to sing with his own, is imaginatively identifying the medieval Christian with the captive Jew and so underlining the figurative interpretation of this biblical story. (Godman's solution is to attach lines 3-5 to the refrain, making *resonare* in asyndeton and parallel to *canere*, 6; he places a period after *itaque*).

s.7	The turning point of the poem: the announcement of the fulfillment, in the form of praise for the Trinity, of the request for a *dulce carmen*. Gottschalk wrote a treatise on the Trinity (*De Trinitate*). This announcement is marked by a change in the refrain.
1	**omnimode:** adverb < *omnimodus*, "of every sort"; "definitely, certainly."
2	**egregie:** vocative of *egregius*.
3-4	Cf. the Creed: *Credo in unum Deum, Patrem omnipotentem ... et in unum Dominum, Jesum Christum Filii Dei unigenitum ... et in Spiritum Sanctum, Dominum et vivificantem, qui ex Patri Filioque procedit ...*
4	**procedente:** CL *procedenti* (cf. *Linguistic Note*, Orthography 1), dative. *Procedente ex utroque* refers to the Holy Spirit; *utroque:* "each of two," i.e., "both." There was major theological debate in the Carolingian period about the "procession of the Holy Spirit"; the western church favored the insertion of *filioque* into the Creed (cf. above on s.7.3-4), while the eastern church opposed the phrase.
6	**ultronee:** adverb < *ultroneus*, "voluntarily." This line introduces a series of varying but similar refrains in ss. 8-12; s. 13.6 is exceptional.

s.8.2	**paraclite:** < Greek παράκλητος, "a person called to one's aid, an advocate"; used in the New Testament to refer to the Holy Spirit as intercessor or comforter.
3	**trine:** < *trini -ae -a* (usually plural), "three at a time, triune."
6	**spontanee:** adverb < LL and ML *spontaneus*, "spontaneously."

s.9.1 **diuscule:** diminutive adverb < *diu*, "for some little time" (Godman).

2 **hoc in mari:** See above on s.1.4-5.

3 **annos ... duos:** accusative of duration of time.
nempe: with *nosti* (4), "without doubt, of course."

4 **nosti:** contracted perfect of *nosco (novisti)*, "you know."
fore: = *esse*, as often in ML. The present tense with expressions of duration of time indicates action begun in the past but continuing into the present.
iam iamque: expresses the imminence of an action (*OLD*), "at this very moment."

5 **miserere:** singular imperative of the deponent *misereor*, "pity."

6 **humillime:** superlative adverb of *humilis*, "very humbly."

ss.10-12 For the recent discovery of these stanzas, see **Ms.** above.

s.10.1 **facinore:** ablative with *plenus*, "full of sin."

3-4 **pleniorem ... pietatem:** Understand "than mine."

3 **sectae:** "following, retinue"; "sect" (*MLLM*). *Sectae verae* = "your true followers" (Godman).

4 **pietatem:** = "piety, faith."

s.11.1 **piissime:** < *pius*, here "most merciful." In both CL and ML "pious," therefore "faithful, devout"; note that "piety" towards one's inferiors, e.g., a suppliant, = "pity " (which also derives from *pietas*). There may be a suggestion that human *pietas* (s.10.4) should be accorded divine *pietas* (s.11.3).

2 **miserere:** See above on s.9.5.

3 **pietatis:** genitive dependent on *memorare* (5), parallel to *famuli* (4).
rector: "ruler."

3-4 Cf. *Luke* 1.54 (of God remembering his own mercy): *Suscepit Israel puerum suum, / Recordatus misericordiae suae.*

5 **memorare:** comes to mean "remember" in ML; the genitive construction is perhaps on the analogy of *memini*.

6 **prono:** See above on s.3.4.

s.12.1-2 At the final point of his prayer, Gottschalk breaks the regular caesura pattern of the first two lines of the stanza.

3 **magis:** "more," i.e., "longer."

4 **flatus alme:** of the Holy Spirit (cf. *O mi custos* s.68.3, *OBMLV* #90.7-8). *Almus*, "fostering, kindly," is a favorite adjective of Gottschalk's.

s.13.1-2 The reinvestigation of the Angers ms. (see above) and the discovery of the correct text here (*situs hac in regione*) ended the concept of this poem as sent from exile to a friend elsewhere, in answer to that friend's request. The poem in fact ends with Gottschalk and his "little son" (*pusione*) joining in a song of praise to the Trinity.

3   **psallam:** < *psallo,* lit. "play on the cithara."

3-4   **die ... nocte:** See above on s.4.3.

5   At the end of the poem, Gottschalk has redefined the nature of a true *carmen dulce* (Klopsch, pp. 92-4); cf. s.1.3.

No. 8
Sedulius: Aut lego vel scribo

Aut lego vel scribo, doceo scrutorve sophian:
    obsecro celsithronum nocte dieque meum.
Vescor, poto libens; rithmizans invoco musas;
    dormisco stertens: oro Deum vigilans.
Conscia mens scelerum deflet peccamina vitae: 5
    parcite vos misero, Christe, Maria, viro.

Commentary

This autobiographical poem, based on classical models of epigram and
self-description reshaped as Christian prayer (*oratio*), has as its most
immediate classical prototype (pseudo) Martial *Anthologia Latina* 1.26 (ed.
Riese): *Rure morans quid agam, respondeo pauca, rogatus. / Mane deos oro
... / Deinde lego Phoebumque cio Musamque lacesso. / Hinc oleo corpus
fingo mollique palaestra / Stringo libens. animo gaudens et fenore liber /
Prandeo, poto, ludo, lavo, cano, ceno, quiesco ...*
    Its author, Sedulius Scottus (d. after 874), was one of several Irish
poets on the continent in the eighth and ninth centuries and a writer of
grammatical treatises, a *Liber de rectoribus Christianis,* and courtly poems
to the emperors Lothar, Charles the Bald, and Louis the German. He is
most noteworthy for his humorous and allusive verses demanding patronage
from the bishops Hartgar and Franco of Liège, a form of poetic request more
typical of the eleventh and twelfth centuries. Piety and learning vie as his
chief interests (he describes himself and his friends as *doctos grammaticos
presbiterosque pios*, Godman #46.14), closely followed by an enthusiasm
for wine and lamb.
    Meter: Quantitative; elegiacs. Correct syllabic quantities (though the
quantity of the i of sophian is doubtful). No rhyme, though Sedulius tends
to place assonances at the ends of the two halves of the pentameter. No
elision.
    Bibliography: Godman, pp. 53-6, 282-3; *OBMLV* #94; *Poetae
Latini Aevi Carolini*, v. 3, p. 225; Raby, *SLP*, v.1, pp. 242-247.

1   **aut ... vel:** in ML can = *et ... et,* "both ... and."
         scrutor: "search, investigate (a subject)."
         sophian: "wisdom" (< Greek σοφία); a Greek accusative: the
         term probably implies not only a knowledge of scripture but also
         knowledge of the classics. Sedulius prides himself on a knowledge
         of Greek (*SLP,* v.1, p. 246), calls himself the Muse's *miles
         sophiae praeditus armis* (*Poetae Latini Aevi Carolini*, v.3, p. 211),
         repeatedly calls himself and his friends *sophos* or *sophicos,* and
         declares that God intends man to be *cupidus et appetens ...*

religionis et sapientiae (quoted in Raby, *SLP*, v.1, p. 242; see above for his self-description as grammarian and priest).

2   **obsecro:** "pray."

celsithronum: epithet of God, "high-throned." The compound adjectives typical of LL and ML (see *Linguistic Note*, Adjectives 1), are recurrent in Sedulius' poetry, e.g., *septimplex, doctiloquax, dulciflua, flavicoma.*

nocte ... die: See *Linguistic Note* (Cases 2).

3   **poto libens:** Sedulius' references to wine are colorful; he prefers wine to beer (*Poetae Latini Aevi Carolini*, v.3, p.177), and utilizes this subject for humor, classical allusion, and punning, e.g., *Nos, fratres, modicum vini modiumve bibamus, / Bachicus in cunctis sit modus aut modius* (Godman #48.31-2). *Libens:* "willingly, gladly."

rithmizans: verb formed from *rhythmus (rythmus)*, in CL "rhythm," in ML "poem"; here, "writing poetry." Cf. Sedulius' use of *cytharizans*, Raby, *SLP*, v.1, p. 243.

4   **dormisco:** an inceptive made from *dormio*; not CL; probably = "sleep," not "fall asleep" (cf. *Linguistic Note*, Vocabulary 4).

5   Cf. Ovid *Fasti* 4.311: *conscia mens recti famae mendacia risit.*

peccamina: ML "sins"; cf. CL peccatum. See *Linguistic Note* (Vocabulary 3).

6   **parcite:** "be merciful (to)"; + dative.

vos: vocative, with the vocatives *Christe* and *Maria.*

No. 9
Andecavis abas

Andecavis abas esse dicitur, s.1
ille nomen primi tenet hominum;
hunc fatentur vinum vellet bibere
super omnes Andechavis homines.
 Refr. Eia eia eia laudes,
  eia laudes dicamus Libero.

Iste malet vinum omni tempore; s.2
quem nec dies nox nec ulla preterit,
quod non vino saturatus titubet
velut arbor agitata flatibus.
 Refr.

Iste gerit corpus inputribile s.3
vinum totum conditum ut aloue,
et ut mire corium conficitur,
cutis eius nunc con vino tinguitur.
 Refr.

Iste cupa non curat de calicem s.4
vinum bonum bibere suaviter,
set patellis atque magnis cacabis
et in eis ultra modum grandibus.
 Refr.

Hunc perperdet Andechavis civitas, s.5
nullum talem ultra sibi sociat,
qui sic semper vinum possit sorbere;
cuius facta, cives, vobis pingite!
 Refr.

Commentary

This is a drinking song, probably written by a cleric since its author needed a smattering of education however poor. It is a rare example, for its period, of secular Latin song; Raby suggests that it is evidence for a continuous tradition of secular Latin songs. The evidence for its date can be deduced only from that of the one ms. in which it is preserved; its provenance is uncertain. Was it written by a light-hearted monk of Italy (the origin of its ms.) or France (*Andecaves* is presumably modern Angers), or was this a song from the secular world copied down illicitly into a monastic collection? It contains a certain amount of the religious parody that is very typical of drinking songs of the later Middle Ages (see P. Lehmann, *Die Parodie im Mittelalter*, Munich, 1922, pp. 174 ff., and no. 30 in this collection). "The Latin is as bad as it can be, that is to say, it is properly adapted to the theme" (Raby, *SLP*, v.1, p. 217).

    Ms.: This poem is preserved in a ninth century ms. (Cod. XC (85) f. 68) in the Biblioteca Capitolare in Verona, Italy.

    Meter: Rhythmical. The pattern of each stanza: 4 x (4p + 7pp) + *Refr.*: 8p + 10pp (if *eia* is scanned as two syllables, cf. *OLD* and Greek εἶα; Raby thinks *eia* scans as three syllables so the refrain lines would also have eleven syllables). *Sorbere* s.5.3 is incorrectly scanned; confusion between the second and third conjugations was frequent in ML. Though there is no rhyme, there are some examples of assonance, perhaps intentional, between line ends (s.3.1-2, s.3.3-4, s.5.3-4) and between caesura and line ends (s.1.4, s.4.3). No elision.

    Bibliography: *OBMLV* #72; *Poetae Latini Aevi Carolini* v.4, p. 591; Raby, *SLP*, v.1, pp. 217-8; G. Vecchi, *Poesia Latina Medievale*, Parma, 1952, pp. 72-3, p. 364.

s.1.1   **Andecavis abas:** "abbot of Angers." *Andecaves* is presumably modern Angers (in the province of Anjou in central France); the *Andecavi* were a Gallic tribe in this area. For *abbas* (this spelling is more correct; New Testament Greek < the Hebrew word for father) see *Linguistic Note* (Vocabulary 2).

        esse dicitur: "there is said to be"; this abbot is legendary.

2   **primi:** genitive dependent on *nomen* and governing *hominum:* the whole phrase = Adam.

3   **hunc...bibere:** "they say he has a desire for wine" (*OBMLV* #72 *ad. loc.*). The author has mistakenly chosen to follow *fatentur* with a substantive subjunctive clause (*ut* to be understood with *vellet*), though by the accusative *hunc* an indirect statement seems to have been originally intended. (Cf. *Linguistic Note*, Subjunctive).

4   **super:** "more than."

        Andechavis: Note the variation, even in the same word in the same ms., in the use of h; cf. *Linguistic Note* (Orthography 7).

Refr.   **eia...Libero** = the refrain, particularly suitable to a drinking song.

        eia: "hurrah." See below on No. 10.41; for its scansion, see above, **Meter.**

        dicamus: hortatory subjunctive.

        Libero: *Liber* was an alternate name for the god of wine, Bacchus; the pun of *liber* ("free") and *Liber* ("wine") was a favorite one (e.g. Sedulius Scottus, *Poetae Latini Aevi Carolini*, v.3, p.198: *hic est libertas, Liber hic liberat omnes* ...), and may be intended here.

s.2.1   **iste:** See *Linguistic Note* (Pronouns 1).

            malet: "likes" (an unclassical use of *malo*). Cf. *Linguistic Note* (Tenses 2).

2   **quem:** = *et eum;* a relative pronoun replacing a demonstrative is used to connect two independent sentences or clauses (called a connecting relative).

            preterit: CL *praeterit* ("pass by, go past"); cf. *Linguistic Note* (Orthography 1).

3   **quod non:** used for *quin* ("but that"), as often in ML; *quin* (*quod non*) governs the subjunctive in clauses after negated expressions of hindering, doubting, or delaying.

            saturatus: perfect passive participle of *saturare*, "fill, drench, saturate."

            titubet: < *titubare*, "to walk unsteadily (especially from drunkenness), stagger."

4   The simile may represent a touch (or parody) of classical learning (e.g. Horace, *Carm.* 1.9.12: *nec veteres agitantur orni*).

s.3.1   **gerit:** "has (physical or mental qualities, etc.)."

            inputribile: LL *imputribilis*, "incapable of decay."

2   **conditum:** perfect passive participle < *condio*, "seasoned, flavored."

            ut: "like, as"; postponed conjunction: translate before *vinum.*

            aloue: ablative, and an eccentric spelling, of *aloe*, "aloe plant," apparently used to season wine.

3   **mire:** probably < *mirr(h)is,* "an aromatic herb," since the poet seems to intend an ablative; possibly confused with *myrrha* or *murra* (myrrh, "an aromatic gum"); the substance was presumably used in preparing hides.

            corium: "hide, leather."

            conficitur: here, "prepare."

4   **con:** a misspelling of the CL *cum* ; cf. modern Italian *con*, "with."

            tinguitur: "wet, soak."

s.4.1   **cupa:** "cask, barrel"; subject, with *iste*, and descriptive of the abbot.

            de calicem: "from a cup" (< *calix*, "drinking cup"). In CL *de* is not followed by the accusative. The poet switches to simple ablatives in 4.3 and to *in* + the ablative in s.4.4. (Cf. *Linguistic Note*, Prepositions).

2   **suaviter:** "agreeably, pleasantly."

3   **set:** = *sed.*

            patellis: "dishes."

            cacabis: "cooking pots."

4   **ultra modum:** "excessively."

            grandibus: in LL and ML, "big."

s.5.1   *Si* is missing: "if the city of Angers loses him" (*OBMLV* # 72 *ad. loc.*); cf. the omission of *se* ("if") possible in modern Italian.

     perperdet: a compound made < *perdo* ; cf. *Linguistic Note* (Vocabulary 4).

2   **ultra:** "subsequently, afterwards."

     sibi sociat: "attach to itself"; in CL *sociat* would be future, if in fact a future more vivid condition is intended by *(si)...perperdet.*

3   **possit:** subjunctive in a relative clause of characteristic or result (it is often hard to distinguish between the two).

     sorbere: < *sorbeo,* "drink up, absorb." (See **Meter** for the scansion).

4   **cuius:** connecting relative in place of a demonstrative (i.e., *eius*; see above on s.2.2).

     vobis pingite: "depict for yourselves, describe to yourselves" (i.e., by singing this song).

No. 10
O tu qui servas

O tu, qui servas armis ista moenia,
noli dormire, moneo, sed vigila!

Dum Hector vigil extitit in Troia,
non eam cepit fraudulenta Graecia.

Prima quiete dormiente Troia   5
laxavit Synon fallax claustra perfida.

Per funem lapsa occultata agmina
invadunt urbem et incendunt Pergama.

Vigili voce avis anser candida
fugavit Gallos ex arce Romulea.   10

[Eius clangore Marcus consul Manlius
excitus primus, vir bello egregius,

umbone Gallum iam in summo positum
ictum in praeceps deturbat miserrimum.

Avis haec vigil, salus viris plurima   15
Capitolinis, sed Gallis nequissima.]

Pro qua virtute facta est argentea
et a Romanis adorata ut dea.

Nos adoremus celsa Christi numina;
illi canora demus nostra iubila!   20

Illius magna fisi sub custodia
haec vigilantes iubilemus carmina!

Divina, mundi rex Christe, custodia,
sub tua serva haec castra vigilia.

[Tu murus tuis sis inexpugnabilis,   25
sis inimicis hostis tu terribilis!]

Te vigilante nulla nocet fortia,
qui cuncta fugas procul arma bellica.

Tu cinge nostra haec, Christe, munimina,
defendens ea tua forti lancea.   30

[Santa Maria, mater Christi splendida,
haec cum Iohanne teothocos impetra.

Quorum hic sancta venerantur pignora
et quibus ista sunt sacrata limina.]

Quo duce victrix est in bello dextera   35
et sine ipso nihil valent iacula.

Fortis iuventus, virtus audax bellica,
vestra per muros audiantur carmina.

Et sit in armis alterna vigilia,
ne fraus hostilis haec invadat moenia.   40

Resultet echo: "comes, eia vigila!"
Per muros "eia!" dicat echo: "vigila!"

Commentary

This is a song written by a learned, presumably clerical writer in
Modena in the last decades of the ninth century, which presents a striking
mixture of classical and biblical learning and allusion but which is most
noteworthy for its vivid quality of actuality. The poem makes specific
reference to a chapel consecrated to the Virgin and John the Baptist (see lines
31-4) and to the walls of Modena (lines 1, 24, etc.); it was probably sung
each night by clerics, perhaps joined by the guards of the walls, in a service
calling for divine protection before the watch took up its duties (Roncaglia,
p. 46). This purpose explains the combined liturgical and military character
of the call for *vigilia*: night offices (*vigiliae*) were a frequent type of church
service in the early Middle Ages, originating no doubt from Biblical
admonitions such as *Vigilate et orate* (*Matthew* 26.40) and *Beati servi illi
quos cum venerit Dominus invenerit vigilantes* (*Luke* 13.35-7); further,
during the same period, all citizens, including clerics, were expected to guard
the city walls (*vigiliae murorum*) on a regular basis (cf. a letter quoted by
Roncaglia, p. 35, in which Gregory the Great protests against those trying
to escape this duty ... *omnes compellantur, quatenus, cunctis vigilantibus,
melius auxiliante Domino, civitatis valeat custodia procurari*). During this
period in north Italy, there were repeated threats of Hungarian invasion. It
was probably against this danger that the walls of Modena were built or
strengthened by Bishop Leodoinus, as indicated by the epigram written into
the Modena ms. by hand no. 4, and against this danger that the Modenese
called for watchfulness and for divine protection. The military and religious
character of this poem is very much in keeping with an age of dissolution of

central authority and the consequent transference to local bishops of extensive civil and military powers.

Ms. This poem is preserved in only one ms. (Ord I, num.4) in the Biblioteca Capitolare of the cathedral of Modena, in northern Italy. This ms. gives the poem with a number of interpolations (additions) and corrections and in four different "hands" (handwritings). Hand no. 1 (the oldest in date, shortly after 881) copied out in order all the text as given here with the exception of lines 11-16. Even in this first copy of the text there are, most scholars think, two interpolations into the poem as originally composed: lines 25-6 are considered additions because they do not end in the usual assonance -a; lines 31-34 are suspect because their two subjects, the Virgin and John, are felt to be inconsistent with *quo duce*, lines 35, which refers back to the subject of lines 29-30, Christ. To consider these lines of Hand no.1 interpolations may be to expect too much consistency of grammar and rhyme in a poem of this period and type. Lines 11-16 are squeezed onto the same page, but are in a different hand, no. 4, which also made corrections in this poem and another in the same ms., and added a brief epigram of historical interest. This hand no. 4, though the latest in date of writing, is probably incorporating material earlier than that of hands 2 and 3; the writer was clearly copying material from another ms. which, in Roncaglia's opinion, was probably the same as the original source ms. used by hand 1. Hands 2 and 3 make further additions to the poem, which are clearly out of keeping with the original work and are therefore omitted from the text given here.

Meter: Rhythmical. The pattern: 2 x (5p + 7pp). (The line is modeled on the classical quantitative iambic trimeter). As the ms. divides the lines into pairs, this pattern has been followed. Possibly the song was at one time structured in 6 line stanzas, as only the music for the first 6 lines has been preserved by the ms. (Roncaglia, p.18) as if it were to be sung in repeated stanzas. Rhyme: rudimentary and typical of early experiments with rhyme. Many lines end only with assonance in -a. In two lines (25-6; see above, **Ms.**) there is (one-syllable) rhyme between the caesura and line ends, an effect which became increasingly popular later in the Middle Ages (Norberg, *Introduction*, p. 41); the difference in quantity of vowels (here of the long and short i's) was often ignored in rhyming by medieval poets. In four lines (11-16; cf. **Ms.**) there is uncertain two-syllable rhyme at the line ends.

Bibliography: Godman, pp. 71-2, 324-7; *Poetae Latini Aevi Carolini*, v. 3, pp. 703-5; A. Roncaglia, 'Il "Canto delle scolte modenesi",' *Cultura neolatina* 8 (1948) 5-46, 205-22; Raby, *SLP*, v.1, pp. 289-90.

1   Cf. Virg. *Aen.* 2.506: *Tu ... moenia serva.*
        ista: "these"; cf. *Linguistic Note* (Pronouns 1).

2   **noli dormire:** a negative command, "don't sleep."
        vigila: < *vigilare*, "to stay awake (at night), be watchful."

3-8	The fall of Troy, taken from Virgil *Aeneid* Book 2; note especially lines 258-9 and 261-2: ... *pinea furtim / laxat claustra Synon ... and ... demissum lapsi per funem / invadunt urbem ...*
3	**vigil:** "awake, watchful, vigilant."
	extitit: < *ex(s)tare*, "exist (in a given manner or condition), be."
4	**Graecia:** "Greeks"; cf. *Linguistic Note* (Nouns 3). The poet of this song favors such abstracts, cf. 37, 40.
5	**Prima quiete:** ablative of time, "in the first quiet of the night," with the ablative absolute *dormiente Troia.* This is a very Virgilian expression, cf. *Aen.* 2.268, 8.407.
6	**laxavit:** "undo (doors, bolts, etc.)."
	Synon: The Greek in *Aeneid* Book 2 who tricks the Trojans into bringing the Wooden Horse inside the walls of Troy, and then at night secretly lets out the hidden Greeks.
	claustra: "bolt, bar," but also "confining space, prison"; used to describe the Trojan Horse and its bolts that enclose the Greeks.
	perfida: a "transferred epithet" that grammatically modifies *claustra* but in sense modifies *Synon.*
7	**lapsa:** perfect participle < *labor, labi,* "slip, slide (down)."
	occultata agmina: refers to the Greeks hidden in the Horse.
8	**Pergama:** neuter plural, "citadel of Troy."
9-18	A scene from early Roman history, to contrast with that from the story of Troy. Geese on the Capitoline hill, awakened by the Gauls scaling the walls (*ca.* 390 B.C.), by their uproar woke M. Manlius who roused the city and saved the citadel. Lines 9-10 and 17-18 are taken from Virg. *Aen.* 8.655-6 (*Atque hic auratis volitans argenteus anser / porticibus Gallos in limine adesse canebat*) with phrases from Ovid (*vigili voce, Metamorphosis* 2.508) and Lucretius (*Romulidarum arcis servator condidus anser,* 4.682). The adjective *argenteus* in Virgil arises from the fact that the scene is depicted on the shield made by Vulcan and given to Aeneas. A later commentator (quoted by Roncaglia, p. 20), clearly read by the author of this poem, attributed the adjective to the color of the bird and to the (perhaps dubious) fact that a silver goose was erected on the Capitoline in honor of the goose who announced the Gallic approach (cf. lines 17-8); the medieval poet has presumably added the idea of idolatrous worship of the goose's statue. Lines 11-16 (see **Ms.**) follow with extreme closeness Livy's account of the same episode (5.47): *Anseres non fefellere ... namque clangore eorum ... excitus, M. Manlius, qui triennio ante consul fuerat, vir bello egregius ... .Gallum qui iam in summo constiterat umbone ictum deturbat.* For lines 17-18 see also idolatrous sacrilege in the Bible, e.g., *De caelo locutus sum vobis: non facietis deos argenteos, neque facietis deos aureos ... (Exodus* 20.22-23, quoted with other Biblical texts by Roncaglia, p. 33).
10	**fugavit:** "put to flight" (to be distinguished from *fugere*).

arce Romulea: "the citadel of Romulus," i.e., the Capitoline hill.

12 **excitus:** < *excio,* "wake up, rouse."
bello: ablative of specification with *egregius* ("outstanding, distinguished").

13 **umbone:** "with his shield"; ablative of means with the perfect passive participle *ictum* (14).
in summo: "on the top of the hill."

14 **ictum:** perfect passive participle from *icere,* "strike."
in praeceps: "headlong."
deturbat: "knock, cast down."

15 **Avis:** Sc. *erat.*
salus: "salvation, saviour" (with religious connotations).
viris: dative, modified by *Capitolinis* (16).

16 **nequissima:** superlative of *nequam,* "bad, evil."

17 **qua:** the relative used as a connective, i.e., a relative pronoun placed at the beginning of an independent sentence or clause to connect it with a preceding sentence or clause; translate as a demonstrative: "for this brave deed."
facta est: Sc. *avis.*

18 **adorata:** Sc. *est* from the previous line.
ut: "as."

19 **adoremus:** hortatory subjunctive (cf. *demus* 20, *iubilemus* 22, *sis* 25-6, etc.).
numina: poetic plural.

20 **illi:** refers to Christ.
iubila: < *iubilus* or *iubilum,* "shouts of joy, song of joy, hymn" (*MLLM*).

21 **illius ... custodia:** The immediate reference is to the need for Christ's protection in very actual circumstances, but the metaphorical use of the *militia Christi,* according to which the Christian life is a battle, Christ the general, and the devil the enemy, was frequent. For the language of 21-24, cf. *Psalms* 126.1: *Nisi Dominus custodierit civitatem, / Frustra vigilat qui custodit eam.*
fisi: perfect participle < *fidere,* "trust in, rely on"; *fidere* becomes deponent in the perfect system.
magna ... sub custodia: See *Linguistic Note* (Prepositions); in CL dative or ablative follows *fidere.*

23-4 There are various possible interpretations. (1) *divina ... custodia* is a vocative addressed to Christ and *sub tua ... vigilia* is ablative of instrument; (2) *divina custodia* is an ablative of instrument (taking *sub tua vigilia* as another ablative of instrument despite variation in the use of the preposition); (3) *divina ... custodia / sub tua* is the ablative phrase and *vigilia* is neuter plural of the adjective *vigil,* modifying castra. (1) is the preferred interpretation. (For the ablative of instrument, cf. *Linguistic Note,* Prepositions 2).

25-6	See above **Ms.** for the possible interpolation of these lines, and **Meter** for the rhyme. For the imagery see on 21.
25	**tuis:** "for your followers."
	inexpugnabilis: "impregnable."
27	**Te vigilante:** ablative absolute.
	fortia: "violence, power"; see *Linguistic Note* (Nouns 4).
28	**fugas:** See above on 10.
29	**munimina:** "defences."
31-4	See above **Ms.** for the possible interpolation of these lines. A note inserted in this same ms. states that a chapel to Christ, the Virgin, and St. John was founded near the city walls on July 26, 881.
32	**haec ... impetra:** literally, "obtain these (things) by entreaty," i.e., "intercede for these things" (Godman).
	teothocos: "mother of God"; nominative feminine, < Greek θεοτόκος; cf. *Linguistic Note*, Orthography 7. Hand no. 4 wrote this word into the text over an erasure of *baptista haec*.
33-4	**Quorum ... quibus:** refer to Mary and John; connecting relative, cf. on 17.
33	**venerantur:** passive; *venero(r)* can be either an active or depondent verb.
	pignora: "relics."
34	**limina:** "threshold", i.e., the chapel. This is an emendation; the ms. has *numina*, which would have to mean "sacred images" (Roncaglia, p. 22).
35	**Quo duce:** ablative absolute in which a noun (*duce*) takes the place of the participle; refers to Christ (29).
	dextera: "right hand," i.e., "soldiers."
37	**iuventus, virtus:** abstract nouns for concrete, i.e., "young men," "brave (men)."
39	**sit ... alterna vigilia:** " may the watch alternate."
40	The line is modeled on Livy ... *ne fraus hostilis vagos exciperet* 5.41, which occurs a few chapters before the episode of the Capitoline geese.
	invadat: "seize" in ML.
41	**Resultet:** "resound."
	eia: an exclamation (also spelled *heia*), expressing various attitudes, e.g. deprecation, concession, astonishment, and, as here, urgency (*OLD*); perhaps "come now"; Godman translates as "hail." Cf. Virg. *Aen.* 9.37: *Scandite muros, hostis adest, eia!*

No. 11
Advertite omnes populi

1a
Advertite,
omnes populi,
ridiculum
et audite, quomodo
Suevum mulier
et ipse illam
defraudaret.

1b
Constantie
civis Suevulus
trans equora
gazam portans navibus
domi coniugem
lascivam nimis
relinquebat.

2a
Vix remige
triste secat mare,
ecce subito
orta tempestate
furit pelagus,
certant flamina,
tolluntur fluctus,
post multaque exulem
vagum littore
longinquo Nothus
exponebat.

2b
Nec interim
domi vacat coniux;
mimi aderant,
iuvenes secuntur,
quos et inmemor
viri exulis
excepit gaudens
atque nocte proxima
pregnans filium
iniustum fudit
iusto die.

3a
Duobus
volutis annis
exul dictus
revertitur.
Occurrit
infida coniux
secum trahens
puerulum.
Datis osculis
maritus illi
"De quo," inquit, "puerum
istum habeas,
dic, aut extrema
patieris."

3b
At illa
maritum timens
dolos versat
in omnia.
"Mi," tandem,
"mi coniux," inquit,
"una vice
in Alpibus
nive sitiens
extinxi sitim.
Inde ergo gravida
istum puerum
damnoso foetu
heu gignebam."

4a
Anni post hec quinque
transierunt aut plus,
et mercator vagus
instauravit remos;
ratim quassam reficit,
vela alligat
et nivis natum
duxit secum.

4b
Transfretato mari
producebat natum
et pro arrabone
mercatori tradens
centum libras accipit
atque vendito
infante dives
revertitur.

5a	Ingressusque domum ad uxorem ait: "Consolare, coniux, consolare, cara: natum tuum perdidi, quem non ipsa tu me magis quidem dilexisti.	5b	Tempestate orta nos ventosus furor in vadosas sirtes nimis fessos egit, et nos omnes graviter torret sol, at il- le nivis natus liquescebat."
6	Sic perfidam Suevus coniugem deluserat; sic fraus fraudem vicerat: nam quem genuit nix, recte hunc sol liquefecit.		

Commentary

This song (known as "Modus Liebinc") is a popular tale in sequence form, probably datable to the tenth century; it was to be sung to the melody (*modus*) of a man named Liebinc. The story appears in the Old French fabliau "L'enfant qui fu remis au soleil" and also in several later, Latin versions. Dronke (pp. 147 ff.) sets it in the tradition of the fabliau ("amusing stories of deception and outwitting, especially of a sexual kind"), which he explains as not limited to the tales of this type written in octosyllabic couplets in France between 1200 and 1350 (the normal scholarly limitation of the term) but as a recurrent form of literary expression of various periods, styles, and languages. Following Per Nykrog's theory (*Les Fabliaux*, Kobenhavn, 1957) of the fabliau as arising from courtly literature as a parody of courtly ideals, he believes this song was written for a probably aristocratic audience by a learned author, who deliberately cast this ribald popular tale into a refined style. There are several touches of religious parody. The parallelism of theme and language between the half-stanza pairs that is typical of the sequence appears here particularly through the contrast and confrontation of husband and wife. If sequences at this period were predominantly religious, this too may have had a parodic effect.

Ms. This song is found in the "Cambridge Songs," a collection of secular and religious songs in a ms. (Gg. 5.35; C) now in the University Library, Cambridge, England. The collection is generally thought to have been made for a well-educated German prelate about the middle of the eleventh century, and gives a surprising picture of the variety of the lyrical repertoire at this period: hymns and sequences; celebratory songs for secular rulers and bishops; didactic songs; songs about nature or music; classical poems set to music; humorous narrative songs (like *Advertite omnes* *populi*); love songs; a dance song. The "Modus Liebinc" is also preserved in two other mss.: 1) Cod. 3610, August. 56.16 (W) in the library at Wolfenbüttel, eleventh century, which is a similar, small collection of songs which includes three other poems from the "Cambridge Songs"; 2) Pal. lat. 1710, fol 16r (P) in the Vatican, tenth-eleventh century.

Meter: In this "archaic" sequence (for the sequence, cf. above, *Medieval Verse Technique*), there are stanza pairs in which the corresponding lines of each stanza (e.g., 1.a.1 and 1.b.1) match almost exactly in number of syllables and in end of line cadences. Exceptions: 5.a/b.6-7; 4.a/b.8. There is a single concluding stanza. No rhyme. No elision.

Bibliography: P. Dronke, "The Rise of the Medieval Fabliau: Latin and Vernacular Evidence," in *The Medieval Poet and his World*, Rome, 1984, pp. 145-165; *OBMLV* #120; Raby, *SLP*, v.1, pp. 291 ff., especially pp. 295-7; K. Strecker, *Die Cambridger Lieder*, Berlin, 1926, pp. 41 ff.

1a.1-2	**Advertite / omnes populi:** These opening lines appear to have both religious and secular connotations. A sequence on the life of St. Paul begins: *Concurrite huc, populi* (quoted by Raby, p. 297); cf. *Isaiah* 34.1: *Accedite, gentes, et audite; / Et populi, attendite.* But the poet may also be beginning "as if he were a fairground performer clamouring for their attention" (Dronke, pp. 149-50). *Advertite* = "notice"; imperative.
3	**ridiculum:** Dronke (p. 152) suggests this may be a term for a well-known type of song. Two other songs in the "Cambridge Songs," (Strecker Nos. 35 and 42) give themselves this name.
4	**quomodo:** "how."
5	**Suevum:** "Swabian." Swabia is a region of southwestern Germany, and was a duchy of southern Germany from the tenth to the mid-thirteenth century.
7	**defraudaret:** See *Linguistic Note* (Subjunctive 1). This verb goes with both subjects (*mulier* and *ipse*) and introduces the theme of mutual deception; cf. the ending 6.1-4.
1b.1	**Constantie:** CL *Constantiae*, modern Constance in southwestern Germany on the Swiss border. Cf. *Linguistic Note* (Orthography 1).
2	**Suevulus:** For the diminutive, cf. *Linguistic Note* (Vocabulary 5).
3	**equora:** CL *aequora*, "seas."
4	**gazam:** "treasure."
7	**relinquebat:** See *Linguistic Note* (Tenses 1).
2a.1	**remige:** < *remex;* "oarsmen" (collective singular).
2	**triste:** modifies *mare*.
	secat mare: Cf. Horace *Carm.* 1.1.14: *pavidus nauta secat mare* and, for *ratim ... reficit* (4.a.5), further in Horace *Carm.* 1.1 (17-18): *mox reficit ratis /quassas.*

4	**orta tempestate:** ablative absolute (see also 5b.1). *Orta:* < *orior*, "rise."
8	**post multaque:** "and after many (troubles)"; *-que* is postponed.
9	**littore:** = *litore*. Locative ablative without a preposition.
10	**Nothus:** CL *Notus*, the south wind; poetically used for wind in general.
11	**exponebat:** Cf. on 2b.7.

2b.2	**vacat:** "be idle."
	coniux: = *coniunx*.
3	**mimi:** "actors," or perhaps "minstrels."
4	**secuntur:** CL *sequuntur;* cf. *Linguistic Note* (Orthography 4).
	quos et: Either the *et* is superfluous (for the rhythm pattern), or *quos* is to be understood as a connective relative.
7	**excepit:** < *excipio*, "meet, greet."
8	**nocte proxima:** "on a following night, soon."
9	**pregnans:** CL *praegnans*, "pregnant."
10	**fudit:** < *fundo*, "pour out, (of a woman) give birth to."

3a.3	**dictus:** "previously mentioned."
5	**occurrit:** "runs up."
8	**puerulum:** See on 1b.2 *Suevulus*.
10	**illi:** dative, refering to the wife.
12	**istum:** The reading of P, *uxor* (vocative), may be preferable (Dronke, p. 148).
13	**extrema:** neuter plural of the adjective used as a noun, "very distressing (things), extreme (suffering)."

3b.4	**in omnia:** "in every direction."
5-6	**mi ... mi:** vocatives, < *meus*; the wife's fear is suggested in the stammering repetition (Dronke, p. 151). *Infit* (the reading of P), instead of *inquit*, is perhaps better as heightening the hesitancy: "she begins to speak."
7	**una vice:** "once."
9	**nive:** < *nix*, "snow."
10	**extinxi:** < *exstinguo*, "extinguish (a fire), kill, quench (a passion, appetite)."
	sitim: "thirst."
11	**inde ... gravida:** Conception through eating or drinking is a common folk-tale motif. The wife's story is unlikely to be a parody of the Virgin birth, as some scholars have thought. *Inde* = "from that."
13	**foetu:** CL *fetu*, "birth."
14	**gignebam:** See on 1b.7. After this stanza, C gives the following:

> *Nam languens amore tuo*
> *consurrexi diluculo*

> *porrexique pedes nuda*
> *per nives et frigora*
> *atque maria rimabar mesta,*
> *si forte ventivola*
> *vela cernerem*
> *aut frontem navis conspicerem.*

This stanza is generally agreed to be interpolated, perhaps through being written in the margin because it could be sung to the same tune and then mistakenly taken as part of the text (Strecker, p. 42; Dronke, *MLREL*, v.1, p. 276).

4a.1   **hec:** CL *haec.*

3   **mercator vagus:** i.e., the husband.

5   **quassam:** < *quatio,* "shake, toss," here, "storm-tossed, shattered."

6   **vela alligat:** i.e., attached new sails, rigged (his ship).

4b.1   **transfretato mari:** redundant: *transfretare* alone = "to cross the sea"; ablative absolute.

2   **producebat:** Cf. on 1b.7.

3   **pro arrabone:** "as payment." Dronke (p. 151) cites evidence from this period (Liutprand of Cremona *Antapodosis* VI.6) that merchants captured and sold young male slaves from northern Europe at extremely lucrative prices.

5   **libras:** literally, "pounds," a standard weight for gold or silver (*MLLM*); perhaps some type of coinage is meant, cf. the Italian *lira.*

5a.2   **ad uxorem:** Note the ML use of a prepositional phrase instead of the CL dative.

3   **consolare:** imperative < *consolor;* "console yourself, be consoled."

7   **me:** ablative of comparison.

5b.3   **vadosas:** "full of shallows."
        sirtes: CL *syrtes,* two areas of sandy flats in the sea between Carthage and Cyrene; generally, "sand bars."

6-7   Here, at the crisis of the story, there is the only exception to the line syllable pattern in the poem.

8   **liquescebat:** < *liquesco,* "melt" (intransitive); cf. *liquefecit* (6.7), "melt" (transitive).

6.1-4   **sic...vicerat:** Dronke suggests there may have been a convention for this type of tale, as there was for later fabliau, of ending with a moral, however sardonic.

3   **deluserat:** pluperfect for perfect (cf. 4, *vicerat*).

5   **quem:** The antecedent is *hunc,* 6.

No. 12
Iam dulcis amica venito

Iam, dulcis amica, venito   s.1
quam sicut cor meum diligo;
ntra in cubiculum meum
rnamentis cunctis ornatum.

bi sunt sedilia strata   s.2
que velis domus parata,
loresque in domo sparguntur
erbeque flagrantes miscentur.

st ibi mensa apposita   s.3
niversis cibis honusta;
bi clarum vinum habundat
quicquid te, cara, delectat.

bi sonant dulces simphonie   s.4
flantur et altius tibie;
i puer et docta puella
anunt tibi cantica pulchra.

lic cum plectro citharam tangit,   s.5
lla melos cum lira pangit;
ortantque ministri pateras
igmentatis poculis plenas."

Non me iuvat tantum convivium   s.6
uantum predulce colloquium,
ec rerum tantarum ubertas
dilecta familiaritas."

Iam nunc veni, soror electa   s.7
pre cunctis mihi dilecta,
ix mee clara pupille
arsque maior anime mee.

.s.p.l. s.8
... que silenti ... .
equenter effugi tumultum
vitavi populum multum."

Ego fui sola in silva   s.9
dilexi loca secreta
igique frequentius turbam
que ... plebis catervam.

Iam nix glaciesque liquescit, s.10
folium et herba virescit,
philomela iam cantat in alto,
ardet amor cordis in antro."

"Karissima, noli tardare, s.11
studeamus nos nunc amare;
sine te non potero vivere,
iam decet amorem perficere.

Quid iuvat differre, electa, s.12
que sunt tamen post facienda?
Fac cita, quod eris factura:
in me non est aliqua mora."

Commentary

This song is a lyrical dialogue between a man and a woman. The assignment of speaker is tentative. Raby gives stanzas 1-5, 7, 10-12 to the man; Bradley agrees with Raby's speaker assignments, but his order of stanzas is 1-7, 10, 8, 9, 11, 12 and he includes the fragmentary stanza 8; Dronke differs in believing the man speaks 6 and the girl follows 9 with 10. The poet skillfully interweaves extensive classical allusions and echoes from the *Song of Songs*; that Biblical text may have suggested the dialogue form to the poet. The complex fusion of sensual and mystical connotations that the typical medieval reader found in the *Song of Songs* has led to much scholarly debate about the meaning of this poem. Dronke insists on the "multivalence" of the language and talks of the "characteristically medieval tension between love as temptation and love as aspiration" ("The Song of Songs and Medieval Love Lyric," p. 223). Wilhelm suggests that the poet is de-allegorizing the language of the *Song of Songs* and setting the emphasis firmly on *this* world.

Ms.: This text is a composite put together from three different mss.: C = Cambridge UL, Gg.5.35, f.438v (the "Cambridge Songs"); V = Vienna Cod. Vindob. 116, f.157v; P = Paris BN, lat. 1118, f.247v. There are three major problems in reconstructing the text: the order of the stanzas (differing in each of the mss.); the assignment of the stanzas to the speakers; the variants in the mss. texts, the most extreme example of which is the omission of some stanzas in each of the mss. The Cambridge Ms. omits stanzas 10 and 11, and is the only ms. to include the fragmentary stanza 8; the order of the stanzas is: 1-3, 5, 4, 9, 8, 6, 12, 7. After the collection was brought from Germany to the monastery of St. Augustine at Canterbury, one of the monks erased parts (mostly the more profane parts) of the song. V (written on the last page of a codex of rhetorical treatises) contains all of the stanzas except 8 and 10; the stanza order is: 1-7, 9, 11,12. P has stanzas

1-5, 9,10, in that order, and thus omits the more obviously erotic stanzas. According to Dronke (*MLREL*) this song was probably sung during the same period both as a sacred *conductus* at St. Martial in Limoges (= the Paris Ms., which omits the more obviously sexual stanzas) and, in a secular context, as a love song. A more recent theory of Dronke's about this song ("The Song of Songs and Medieval Love Lyric") is that there were two separate poems, one sacred and one profane, which should be kept distinct in publication; the sacred version = P; the "seducer's" version = V. The text printed here assumes one long, secular poem which is an artistic whole.

Meter: Rhythmical. There is a rough equality of syllables (9 in most of the lines, but a few have 8 or 10) and no fixed final cadence. The rhymes can be either monosyllabic or disyllabic. Probably no elision. The pattern: 4 x 9º / aabb.

Bibliography: Dennis R. Bradley, "Iam dulcis amica venito," *Mittellateinisches Jahrbuch* 19 (1984) 104-115; Dronke, *MLREL*, v.1, pp. 271 ff.; Dronke, "The Song of Songs and Medieval Love Lyric," in *The Medieval Poet and his World*, Rome, 1984; *OBMLV* #122; Raby, *SLP*, v.1, pp.303-4; K. Strecker, *Die Cambridger Lieder*, Berlin, 1926, pp. 69-73; Wilhelm, pp. 97-102.

s.1 ff. The invitation of lover to girl is to be found in the *Song of Songs* (2.10 ff.): *Surge, propera, amica mea ... et veni ... Surge, amica mea ... et veni ... Vox enim tua dulcis ...* (note the repeated *veni*; cf. *Song of Songs* 4.8 ff., 5.1). Also from the *Song of Songs* are the forms of address: *amica, soror, dilecta, electa;* the spring scene of stanza 10 (*Song of Songs* 2.11-13): *iam enim hiems transiit; imber abiit, et recessit; flores apparuerunt ... vox turturis audita est in terra nostra ...* ; the room (*Introduxit me rex in cubiculum suum* 1.4, cf. 3.4-6. The harlot's invitation to the young man from *Proverbs* 7 (especially 16-18) may have been in the poet's mind; equally present perhaps is Horace's invitation to Venus (*Carm.* 4.1).

1.1 **venito:** future imperative, second person singular. This line, perhaps unintentionally, echoes *venito / tu iam dulcis amor* addressed to the cuckoo in No. 5, *Conveniunt subito cuncti.*

s.2.1 **sedilia:** < *sedile,* "chair."
strata: < *sterno,* "spread (with covers)."
2.2 **velis:** "woven hangings or curtains."
2.4 **herbe:** CL *herbae*; see *Linguistic Note* (Orthography 1). Cf. *simphonie* (4.1) , *tibie* (4.2).
flagrantes: variant form < *fragro,* "smell sweet."

s.3.2 **honusta:** CL *onusta,* "laden." Cf. *Linguistic Note* (Orthography 7); cf. 3.3 *habundat.*

.4.2 **et:** postponed; translate before *inflantur.*

altius: (of sounds) "deep, loud." For the comparative, see *Linguistic Note* (Adjectives 2).

4.3   **docta puella:** Cf. Propertius 1.7.11; 2.11.6; 2.13.11.

4.4   **cantica:** < *canticum*, "song."

s.5.1   **cum:** See *Linguistic Note* (Prepositions 2).

5.2   **melos:** neuter accusative, "song."
lira: ablative, "lyre."
pangit: "plays."

5.3   **pateras:** "drinking cups," while *poculis* , 5.4 = "drinks."

5.4   **pigmentatis:** "spiced"; this is the reading of V, which gives a nine-syllable line. Another version has *diversis*.

s.6.1   **convivium:** "feast."

6.2   **predulce:** CL *praedulce*, "very sweet."
colloquium: "talk, conversation."

6.4   **ut:** "as."
dilecta: This is the reading of V. Strecker conjectured *cara*. The reading of C is *clara* (Bradley defends this as "open, made manifest").
familiaritas: "friendship"; Dronke sees these lines as an outright request for love and therefore too openly encouraging for the girl at this point in the dialogue.

s.7   Bradley points out that as the man begins to speak again, echoes of the *Song of Songs* recur. Note the insistent recurrence of *iam* (7.1) ... *iam* (8.1) that recalls l.1.

7.1   **veni:** imperative.

7.2   **pre:** CL *prae*. Cf. *mee ... pupille* (7.3), *anime mee* (7.4).

7.3   **pupille:** "eye."

7.4   **parsque ... mee:** See, for instance, Horace *Carm.* 1.3.8 (*animae dimidium meae*); Ovid *Ex P* 1.8.2 (*pars animae magna ... meae*); Dronke ("The Song of Songs," p. 224) points out, however, that such phrases became conventional Christian expressions of friendship.

s.8   This fragmentary stanza is found only in C. Bradley defends its separate authenticity by pointing out that in P and V stanzas 8 and 9 are conflated into one (= 9.1-2 + 8.3-4), which probably occurred because the copyist's eye, influenced by similarity of content, slipped from 9.2 (this stanza precedes in C) to 8.3. He convincingly assigns it to the man, and to precede stanza 9: the girl's *frequentius* 10.3 is picking up *frequenter* 9.3 as well as the more general content; the puzzling perfects (*fui, dilexi* ...) of stanza 9 match those of stanza 8. Bradley (p. 111) suggests that the man is illustrating his love by describing his wandering in the solitary wilds and avoiding men; this is a *topos* of lovers' behaviour. The girl then replies in stanza 9 by saying that she has been behaving in a similar way; this response (and stanza 10, according to the arrangement of the text given here) leads the man to the enthusiasm of stanzas 11-12. Other scholars interpret this stanza as an alternate version, perhaps a different oral tradition, of stanza 9.

8.1-2   The only word any longer to be read in these lines is *silenti*.

.9.4   No word has been found that will accommodate all the letters Strecker identified in the ms. here; Bradley suggests *multam, molestam*, or, perhaps best, *malignam*.
    catervam: "crowd."

.10   There is much debate about the placing and the speaker of this stanza, which is to be found only in P. The imagery seems to develop naturally from that of stanza 9 and to be a delicate expression of the girl's love. Some scholars think that the evocation of spring, often connoting love in medieval lyric, and the almost outright declaration of love in 10.4 suit the male speaker better.

0.2   **folium:** collective singular, "foliage."
0.3   **philomela:** "nightingale" (see above, *Vox philomela,* No. 3).
    in alto: probably, "on high."

.11.1   **Karissima ... noli tardare:** an echo of the prayer to God, *Psalm* 39, in the form used in the Advent liturgy: *Veni, Domine, et noli tardare* (Strecker, p. 71; Dronke, "The Song of Songs," p. 222); if the echo is conscious, the effect would be irreverent or even parodic. *Karissima = carissima. Noli tardare*: "don't be slow."
1.2   **studeamus nos:** hortatory subjunctive; *nos* is nominative.
1.3   **sine ... vivere:** Cf. Ovid: *sine te nec ... vivere possum* (*Amores* 3.11.39).

.12.1   **quid:** "why?"
    differre: "postpone."
2.2   **que:** = *quae*.
    post: adverb.
    facienda: "to be done."
2.3   **cita:** < adjective *citus*, modifying the girl; translate "quickly."
    eris factura: "you will do." *Linguistic Note* (Tenses 4).
2.4   **in me ... mora:** Cf. Virgil: *in me mora non erit ulla* (*Eclogue* 3.52) of a shepherd agreeing to take part in a singing match.